Old Gods, New Druids

First published by O Books, 2009
O Books is an imprint of John Hunt Publishing Ltd., The Bothy, Deershot Lodge, Park Lane, Ropley,
Hants, SO24 0BE, UK
office1@o-books.net
www.o-books.net

Distribution in:	South Africa
	Alternative Books
UK and Europe	altbook@peterhyde.co.za
Orca Book Services	Tel: 021 555 4027 Fax: 021 447 1430
orders@orcabookservices.co.uk	
Tel: 01202 665432 Fax: 01202 666219	Text copyright Robin Herne 2008
Int. code (44)	
	Design: Stuart Davies
USA and Canada	
NBN	ISBN: 978 1 84694 226 6
custserv@nbnbooks.com	
Tel: 1 800 462 6420 Fax: 1 800 338 4550	All rights reserved. Except for brief quotations
	in critical articles or reviews, no part of this
Australia and New Zealand	book may be reproduced in any manner without
Brumby Books	prior written permission from the publishers.
sales@brumbybooks.com.au	
Tel: 61 3 9761 5535 Fax: 61 3 9761 7095	The rights of Robin Herne as author have been
	asserted in accordance with the Copyright,
Far East (offices in Singapore, Thailand,	Designs and Patents Act 1988.
Hong Kong, Taiwan)	
Pansing Distribution Pte Ltd	
kemal@pansing.com	A CIP catalogue record for this book is available
Tel: 65 6319 9939 Fax: 65 6462 5761	from the British Library.

Printed by Digital Book Print

Old Gods, New Druids

Robin Herne

BOOKS

Winchester, UK
Washington, USA

CONTENTS

The author would like to express thanks to:
The current and former members of Clan, who have helped to
shape these lessons over the years;
My partner, Terry, for his support;
The prisoners who have studied the early version of this course;
Dr Mark Williams, for his linguistic and historical advice;
Those members of 'The Druid Network' who provided feedback;
Plus, of course, to the Honey Tongued Lord Himself.

Introduction

Apologies must go to Drew Campbell for drawing so heavily on the title of his excellent work on Greek polytheism[1] for the title of this work. Reading all those Irish sagas about cattle raiding must have affected the balance of my mind, and led me to engage in such shameless literary pilfering!

This book aims to reflect on the nature of the ancient Gods worshipped by the early British and Irish, what we know of the manner in which they were reverenced by those tribes, and how people in the 21st century can relate to them. A grand aim, you might think, but if we don't aim high there's no point in notching the bow (incidentally, one of the weapons which Lucan described Ogmios[2] as carrying!).

This book is a joint effort between a number of people, though most of the writing and grammatical errors have been down to one person ~ which sometimes means that the use of "we" is genuinely collective, and sometimes the royal prerogative only exerted by egomaniacs and queens (it will be left to the reader to guess which one the author is!).

We have met Heathens who felt worn down by having to struggle against the constant assumption that they must be neo-Nazis ~ an assumption made not just by Christians or passing atheists but by plenty of other Pagans too.

Claiming a Celtic spirituality these days also feels pretty exhausting, not to say demoralising. No one (so far) has suggested that we parade around in jackboots... well, except those kinky guys at the pub last Thursday, but let's not go there. Joanna Hautin-Mayer's excellent article ('When is a Celt not a Celt?'[3]) expounds upon the difficult associations between ethnicity, language, culture and spirituality previously outlined in Marion Bowman's notion of Cardiac Celts. If you haven't read either, we recommend doing so!

Some eclectic Pagans and New-Agers claim virtually every and anything as Celtic, whilst some academics seem determined to prove that so few things are Celtic that the tribes can scarcely have had a culture at all. Geneticists and sociologists do battle as to who is "truly" Celtic, and what it even means to be Celtic in the first place. Even amongst those who class themselves as pursuing a mystical path, constant battle rages as to who is more Celtic than thou. Let's not even get into the political factions who seem to think being a Druid requires one to either support the IRA, or hate Romans, or loathe Saxons, or be of certain exclusive bloodstock.

Just as there are a hundred brands of Wicca, so there are endless subsets that come, however loosely, under the banner of Celtic spirituality. There are Celtic Wiccans, Romantic Druids, Revivalist Druids, Gaelic Traditionalists, Celtic Reconstructionists, Tuathans, Senistrognata, Aurrad, Wittans, Druidiactos, Fenians, Dryads, Ueledans and on and on it goes.

This book describes a little of what we do, and why we do it. What we will avoid doing is adding yet another label to the heap, or try to add to the maelstrom by tearing apart other peoples practices. Should you be wondering who "we" are, then we are a small group of people living in East Anglia (for non-British readers, that's on the east coast of England) who are part of a ritual group that has been running since 1993. We devote ourselves to the gods and goddesses reverenced by both the British and Irish tribes some 2000-odd years ago. These are the deities that call to us most strongly. Many of us also reverence deities from other lands and cultures, but do so in rituals separate from the group.

The rituals we perform for these Gods are not historical re-enactments of what the Ancient Britons were getting up to. Firstly, detailed evidence for their rituals is very slim indeed. Secondly, there is no indication of continuity in *their* rituals over time or place. A funeral rite conducted by the Iceni in 50 BCE may well have been quite different from one conducted by the Brigantes in

200 BCE. Instead of trying to replicate a piece of historical whimsy, we are trying to form meaningful relationships with our Gods in the 21st century. The rituals we perform are influenced by several factors ~ what the deity in question want us to do; what we actually have the resources or skills to do; and what has a desirable spiritual impact on us.

The latter factor is important, because we are not slaves mindlessly making obeisance in a one-sided relationship. Not only must the ritual please the deity, but we need to get something out of it too.

Broadly speaking, we perform two main types of ritual. There are celebratory rituals, which usually give thanks for some good thing that has come to pass ~ the beauties of the changing seasons, an important event in a member's life etc. Then there are the magical rituals, performed only sporadically, which are geared at instigating some change in ourselves, or the world around us.

Magical rituals are, for us, a rarity and almost entirely take the form of agreements or pacts with our Gods and other spirits. Many might class them more as prayer than spell casting. Morris Berman, in his 1981 work 'Re-enchantment of the World' wrote,

> The view of nature which predominated in the West down to the eve of the Scientific Revolution was that of an enchanted world. Rocks, trees, rivers, and clouds were all seen as wondrous, alive, and human beings felt at home in this environment. The cosmos, in short, was a place of belonging. A member of this cosmos was not an alienated observer of it but a direct participant in its drama. His personal destiny was bound up with its destiny, and this relationship gave meaning to his life.

For us magic is not about waving wands or conjuring elemental spirits, but about the restoration of the very sense of wonder, belonging and awe that Berman describes.

As well as Gods we also perform rituals geared at communicating with other spirits ~ such as ancestors, the *Sídhe* (sort of nature spirits), the *bocain* (rather like land wights) and so forth.

The pattern of our ceremonies was inspired by looking at the behaviour of the old tribes towards honoured guests. Gods are not invoked, because we feel that, if it wants, anything so powerful will turn up (if it is not there already) whether we ask it or not. Likewise, we do not invoke the spirits of place because they are already there. Rather, we address them. This may seem like semantic quibbling, but there is a mental approach that goes with summoning or calling down a spirit that, in these instances, we feel inappropriate for us. However, some spirits do seem to require a formal invite ~ particularly the souls of the dead.

Once a spirit has been formally greeted various forms of entertainment are laid on. These are fun activities that the spirit has expressed some interest (prior to the ceremony) in experiencing. Examples of things we have done include storytelling, praise poetry, mead brewing, sword fighting, making music, chanting, archery, cooking food and mulling wine, and drag hunting.

Having entertained them, that is when we get down to business. Through meditation, divination, and visionary experiences we establish a link with the spirits in question. They inform us of anything else they want done in future, we may ask for advice on personal matters, interventions (for which a reciprocal gift is made) and so forth. Ardent atheists may well question our sanity at this stage (in the unlikely event that any of them are reading this book), but beware the day when everyone goes completely sane ~ we shall probably all die of boredom the day after!

Once the link is established, a feast is held and the spirits are thanked. If they disappear off into the Otherworld or continue to hover round this one, is entirely down to them.

In terms of annual festivals we hold to the four major Gaelic festivals of *Samhain, Imbolc, Beltaine,* and *Lughnasadh.* Much debate can be seen in books as to exactly what these festivals meant to ancient Celts. We suspect they meant different things to different tribes at different periods, just as the way Christmas is popularly viewed today is quite different from the way it was viewed 500 years ago, even though the central concept remains the same. We doubt there was any definitive meaning to these festivities even in the pre-Christian world. Each year we commune with the Gods and let them guide us as to what they want done at that festival for that year. In 2003 we also held a midsummer ritual down at the beach to honour Manannán mac Lir. There is some evidence of midsummer ceremonies to him being held on the Isle of Man, though the format that he requested did not involve any of the activities mentioned in the Manx records.

In addition to these major festivals, if a spirit puts in a request (completed in triplicate, with at least 28 days notice) then we will hold other festivals on a one-off basis. One April we held a ritual to honour Blodeuwedd, which involved making mead from some of the plants mentioned in her myth, for example.

Sometimes Wiccan friends have asked us how we cast a Circle. As such we don't. However, many traditions have a sort of opening gambit which they do at the start of every ritual ~ either as a means of declaring the place sacred, or to focus the minds of participants, or to psychically cleanse the area of disturbing presences (or all of the above, and a few more reasons besides). In this sense, we are no different. We have no idea what the ancient tribes did at the start of their ceremonies. Even if we did, there is no guarantee we would want to do the same. We have changed our format about a dozen times over, refining it, questioning the validity of doing it this way rather than that etc. The form we have finally settled upon (till the next big change) is to give our thanks to the spirit of the place for letting us ritualise there (having checked in advance that we could do so), to ask the goddess Nemetona to guard the ceremonial space from all unwanted intrusions and to make a series of toasts to the Gods to be honoured in ritual, the ancestors who guide us, and to each other for fellowship and support.

In outdoor rituals we pour libations on the roots of a tree. Indoors, we pour them into a cauldron or bowl that can be emptied later. In either case the tree or the cauldron forms a focal point to the ritual, and we process around it a certain number of times to mark the official start and finish of the ritual. We got his idea from the common practice in Celtic countries of circumambulating a special site. We like it, and the spirits don't seem to mind.

The functions of Druids in the ancient world are much debated, as is the matter of how sensible it is to claim to be a Druid in the modern one. Do we consider ourselves modern counterparts to the ancient Druids? The answer is: sort of. Druids performed many functions for the old tribes. Some of the duties are beyond our league ~ we can't imagine that any of us will ever end up advising monarchs, aside from the occasional queen! However, there are functions that we certainly perform in our daily lives. Some of us teach, some heal the sick, we all perform ritual, commune with the same Gods, give guidance to people who seek it, study Celtic languages, aspire to live honourably, some represent our faith at civic events etc.

The Book of Ballymote (circa 1390), a medieval Irish tome, described various professions as having seven grades. Qualifications were given for each rank. A text called the *Uraicecht na Riar* goes into considerable detail about the seven *Fili* (poet) grades[4] and what had to be learnt to qualify for each level, what privileges each could expect in society etc. No mention was made in this book of the *Druí* or *Fáith* (seer) professional structure, if indeed they had one. By the 14th century there were probably few, if any, Druids left to require a career structure. Without the benefit of a Tardis or a miraculous archaeological discovery, we may never know how the Druids of a thousand years prior to the

Uraicecht organised themselves.

They may have had seven tiers, or three, or a dozen ~ we can but speculate[5]. Though, to root back into pragmatic soil, even if some mystical stone tablet with all the answers on were to be unearthed tomorrow, it would not compel modern polytheists to follow suit. In musing upon the possibilities of the past what we seek is inspiration, not a rigid template to slavishly emulate. What may have worked wonderfully 2000 years ago may not be much use now, and vice versa.

What particularly inspired one Clan member (namely me, and I am now planning a quick exit stage left, pursued by an angry mob) to suggest the seven-tiered system as a working model for our teaching plan was the detailed syllabus of knowledge associated with each layer. A copy of this educational structure may be found in the Appendix. Using the *Fili* grades for inspiration, along with a bit of mystic guidance, we have developed a workable proposal for what a modern day *Druí* might be expected to know at each grade. The reason for doing this is to have something to work towards, effectively creating deliberate pauses in the learning so that students (and teacher alike) can draw breath, reflect on what they have learnt so far, and celebrate their achievements. Such grades have no validity outside of the group, but then they do not need to. Value in the eyes of one's kith is more important than the opinions of strangers.

The scholar R. E. Reynolds, writing for *Speculum* in 1979, suggested that the poet-seers of the 1300's adapted the 'seven-fold with three-subs' model from the Church, which used a similar structure at that time. Other manuscripts from the 14th century described eight grades of noble bards[6] and eight of base bards. The *Bretha Nemed* manuscript gives six types of bard. The names of different grades vary from one text to another, suggesting that such things may have altered over time and perhaps also place. Prior to this revision the *filid* may have had more or less than seven grades. Indeed, it is possible that the earlier *filid* in different parts of Ireland may have been structured differently from each other. As well as pulling in line with the Church, such a move could also have served to promote some kind of national standardisation of the poetic class.

Strong evidence for Reynolds view is found in a 7th century work called the Crith Gabhlach. This explains that the seven-tier system was set in place to correspond *'with the Church grades, for any grade that is in the Church, it is right that its corresponding one should be in the túath'*. The extent of this particular numerical symbolism in both Christianity and Judaism seems marked. A quick trawl through a King James Bible yielded assorted references within the Book of Revelation, including the seven seals, seven churches and lots more besides. Plus there are the Seven Deadly Sins and the Seven Cardinal Virtues, of course, and Jehovah rested on the seventh day after creating the world. However, Reynolds saw it as stemming primarily from the Seven Gifts of the Holy Spirit[7] which are alluded to in Isaiah 11: 2-3 and form part of the catechism. None of us in Clan are sufficiently enamoured of Church history to chase the roots of this symbolism any further, but suffice to say seven was (and remains) an important number within Christianity.

Some readers, especially those who have had bad experiences of Christianity, may shy away from anything that smacks of the Church[8]. This is fair enough, but we would suggest that having some form of structure (based on whatever number your heart desires) would be a major help to whoever facilitates the teaching within your group. Those readers who have never attempted to teach a complex topic may not appreciate how frustrating it can be to do so without any sense of order or form.

If you do not fancy a seven-fold format but would nonetheless like a structure with some poetic resonance, then you could emulate OBOD (Order of Bards, Ovates and Druids) by organising your teachings in triads; or maybe you might prefer more manageable pentads to draw a link with the five provinces and the numerous uses of five-fold imagery in the Brehon law codes; or, if you are truly masochistic and want to hike the volume of learning, seek inspiration in the Nine Waves.

At this point some readers might wonder why the influence of Christianity should cause a problem. As such it doesn't, but there are background issues to take into account. Peoples reasons for converting to Pagan religions vary, two common ones being hearing the call of the Old Gods and feeling alienated from both the mainstream religion (Christianity in the UK) and atheism. Of course these two motivations can often exist side-by-side in the same individual. Many modern Pagans view the Church as an oppressive force, and sometimes get caught up in the rather a-historical romance of the supposed Burning Times of the witch-hunting persecutions (which ignores the great likelihood that most of those unfortunate people being hanged or burned were actually Christians who had run afoul of neighbourhood feuds; and even more curiously overlooks all those genuine polytheists persecuted earlier on during the political machinations of Theodosius, King Olaf, Charlemagne and others).

Exaggerated histories aside, Christianity does not have a good track record with its treatment of women or gay people, and its involvement in political imperialism has not endeared it to many people from indigenous cultures. Painful personal experiences can couple with a rosy view of a pre-Christian Golden Age in which bigoted attitudes did not exist (temporarily ignoring the fact that disenfranchisement of women was going on for a long time before Paul walked abroad). A belief in a mythical Good Old Days before sexism, homophobia, dark satanic mills, and all the other bugbears of modern life can lead to an aversion towards Christianity in which it becomes caricatured as the source of all wrong. Myths, incidentally, strike us as being there to inspire us to shape a glorious future rather than to mope passively about a lost past.

As polytheists we might also ask ourselves where Jehovah,

Jesus, Mary, Satan etc sit in our view of the cosmos. Most European polytheists of our acquaintance are quite happy with the idea that Ganesh, Lakshmi, Yü Huang Shang Ti, Erzulie and many other deities exist even if they have never personally encountered them. That the figures of monotheist belief also exist is often verbalised but may not always be reflected on in any great depth. To the polytheist mind a deity like Jehovah or Allah is one god amongst a thousand, rather than the One and Only God. How then are we to take the claims of their being the sole forces in the universe? Some may see these claims as being the political writings of human clerics rather than reflecting the actual views of the deity. Some may regard the deity as some kind of *enfant terrible*[9] making dishonest exaggerations of his own importance. Others may make yet more complex interpretations.

Ancient and modern polytheists can and have incorporated elements of Christian, Islamic and other monotheistic cultures into their spiritual practice without the world grinding to a halt as a result. One might argue that monotheism has become so pervasive in the West that it is now practically impossible not to be influenced by its values, assumptions and social structures regardless of whether one loves it or loathes it. Better to make a conscious choice about how it influences you than to assume one is spiritually radical whilst all the time blindly rehashing the very forces one is trying to get away from.

A modern Druid could attempt to do what people must presumably have done once, many thousands of years ago ~ and start from scratch. She could discard the Welsh and Irish myths as too heavily Christianised, perhaps even rejects words like Druid and Celtic as having far too much baggage, and instead sit beneath a tree and quietly meditate and see what Cernunnos, Danuvia or Brigantia have to say. Such a spiritual practice could endeavour to start again from ground zero. Though it rather assumes that the Gods exist in some Otherworldly realm hermeneutically sealed from the cultural changes in this one.

Some people may well view the Gods as rather like Platonic Forms, perfect ideals that never change and can be accessed now in the identical state they were in 5000 years ago. Within Clan we do not see the Gods as transcendent in another dimension, but as immanent in this one. They are the trees, the rocks, the rivers, the deer herds, the bee swarms, and the human race with all its whims and changes.

Even for those who consider the Gods immutable, the fact that we are not must be addressed. Your mind, dear reader, is the product not only of however many years you have been alive, but also of the countless generations who shaped and sustained the world into which you were born. Whatever the Gods say to us must filter through the prism of our minds, with all its planes and contours formed by religion, politics, history, TV, culture and custom. The way any Divine Revelation might filter through your mind will be different from how it would have been interpreted by the mind of a Coritani tribesman.

To reject the intervening centuries of written mythology in pursuit of a theoretically purer era is also a rejection of those ancestors that adhered to polytheism within that time and who might well guide the living from beyond the grave. The essential nature of the spirituality we are immersing ourselves in is such that we venerate the spirits of place ~ by this we mean not only geographical place, but the chronological place in which we dwell, itself the product of past generations and their beliefs. To discard their thoughts and deeds as tainted would be deeply misguided, and the religious equivalent of sticking ones head in the sand.

A Classics scholar might also highlight the extent to which early Christianity incorporated many of the teachings and practices of the Pagan religions of Greece, Rome, Egypt and elsewhere. So, to some extent, these days we see Wiccans, Druids and other neo-pagans unwittingly using elements of Christian teaching which themselves were often once the teachings of the

Mediterranean Pagan cultures. It all gets a bit confusing!

The old tribes did not lay down a specific ethical code by which to live ~ or, if they did, it did not survive the passage of time. There are books that give sayings and precepts from Scotland, Wales, and Ireland etc. These have all been written down during the Christian period, though some of them may well express sentiments current amongst the Pagan tribes. One of our favourites is the motto attributed to the Fianna, the war band of the warrior-druid Fionn Mac Cumhail: *'Strength in our hands, truth in our hearts, fulfilment on our tongues.'* This made its first written appearance in the 12th century text *Acallam na Senórach*, 'The Colloquy of the Old Men'. The author of that text may have coined the motto, though we prefer to imagine that he was drawing on a maxim that was old even then. Courage, personal integrity, eloquence and a passionate embrace of life ~ what more could we ask? It means that we have to make our own moral judgements about the choices life gives us. For further insights we can study the Brehon laws of old Ireland, though merely because people behaved one way a 1000 plus years ago, is hardly a cause for us to do the same now ~ unless, through reasoned approach, it seems like a wise idea.

Two aspects of the far past that do inspire us are tribalism and *joie de vivre. Anomie* and social isolation seem to be a normal state for far too many people these days. With such a vast population, it is hard to see how we will ever be able to form tribal communities again. However, we do feel that such social unity is vital to our survival as a species. Not to mention our happiness as individuals.

Classical accounts of the Celtic tribes describe a loud bunch with a riotous enjoyment of life. We enjoy being around people who are colourful, funny, forthright, eloquent and sybaritic. Most of the miserable people we know are inhibited, timid, subservient, fearful of seizing life, and seldom getting any pleasure out of it. Passion brings its own problems, but we prefer it to being a colourless shade.

Trees, of course, play a strong role in Celtic religion. Trees are not the only important living things in our faith ~ animals, plants, rocks, rivers. Even humans get a look in every so often! Experience convinces us that humans are far from being the only sentient thing on this planet. Part of our spiritual growth is forming relationships with the other living, thinking creatures around us. One of the common themes in Celtic myth is learning about a thing by becoming it.

We do not regard ourselves as reconstructing an ancient religion, but rather as forming mutually beneficial relationships with a tribe of deities who were once commonly reverenced in this land. A corollary of these relationships is that we also seek to form a link with those long-dead people who also knew these Gods. Their experiences can only better inform ours. We do not try to emulate them, but to learn from their example. We also each have our own blood ancestors who take an interest in us, and those spirits who inhabit the places where we live or visit regularly. Plus some spirits whose interest is not so much in place as in activities. To return, briefly, to the thorny matter of politics ~ what obligations do we have to the modern descendants of the people who used to worship Epona, Lugus, Brigantia and so forth? Learning to speak Welsh will not enable us to conduct rituals in the language of the ancient Druids, in some wonderfully romantic manner. The languages spoken by tribes 2000 years ago are not the same as the ones spoken today, though they are descended from them. However, learning a language will help us to understand the myths more easily, will improve our mental discipline, and helps to preserve something that has been pushed to the edge of extinction.

There is much to be had from preserving sites once sacred to our, or related, deities. We are more than happy to help support the reintroduction of those beasts once held sacred, and the spread of native trees and plants. This we do through planting trees and wild flowers, donating to animal sanctuaries and environmental protection schemes etc.

Matters of cultural preservation, for us, are much more ambiguous. Some people who follow Celtic religions get heavily involved in supporting Celtic political factions, such as supporting the Peace Process in Northern Ireland. Whilst peace is preferable to endless internecine fighting, we have never been entirely clear why we should be supporting groups of frequently violent monotheists who eschew relationships with the Old Gods, and who would probably be deeply antipathetic towards "godless Pagans". Peace yes, party politics no.

Likewise, none of us have ever felt the urge to go on St Patrick's Day parades (though don't let that discourage you from doing so), merely because they are tied to contemporary Celtic culture. We have no desire to celebrate the life of a man who did his best to stamp out the worship of our Gods. We will not support activities merely because they are, in some definite or tenuous manner, Celtic ~ unless they are engaging in something that is beneficial to ourselves, or others on whom our Gods cast a benevolent eye.

What we desire to support, through money or time and effort, is specifically British and Irish polytheist cultures and the diverse eco-system that birthed and sustains them. Those things that are hostile to them will get short shrift, no matter how Celtic they may be.

How To Use This Book

There are quite a few books around now exploring Druidry specifically and "Celtic Spirituality" generally. Some of these books approach the topic from a monotheist viewpoint (often quite a Christianised one), whilst the Analytic Psychology of the late Carl Jung more heavily influences others. Such texts tend to perceive Gods, spirits and other such mysterious entities as archetypes, or aspects of a collective human unconscious. Whilst we do not condemn any of these approaches, we wished to focus this book upon a polytheist understanding of the spiritual traditions that link 21st century people to the deities worshipped in this land thousands of years ago. What this means in a nutshell is that we view our deities and their attendant spirits as real beings with an independent existence outside of us. They are not aspects of greater forces, nor are they the product of human consciousness.

Our assumption is that most people buying a book like this will probably either consider themselves Druids already, or be contemplating it as a possible spiritual discipline. The book can be used for solitary study, or for couples, or groups of people. Your group may be a longstanding one looking for a new direction, or it may be something that only formed last Thursday after one bottle of Chianti too many. In a sense this book is rather like a set of teacher's notes, each chapter providing a lesson. You could read these out to your group, taking lots of time to pause every few paragraphs and discuss. When the weather is good (or even if it isn't, should your health permit) you could go out to the local woods and intersperse reading with meditation, tree hugging, nature walks etc. Field guides to help you identify wild plants, mushrooms, birds etc will prove an invaluable addition.

If no members already speak Gaelic, Welsh, Cornish[10] etc, then you might also be able to lay hands to some tapes or CDs to help get your minds round pronouncing some of the more tongue-twisting words.

Having sessions in which you practice visualisation, chanting, storytelling and other such skills is also important. As a practical suggestion, try doing these things on days separate from the ones in which you use the chapters of this book. We have learnt that trying to do too many activities in one session simply doesn't work.

Each chapter ends with a question section, and it will doubtless prove more interesting and productive to debate these points with other people rather than just musing alone. Perhaps you could have the questions as something to engage with over a drink and some crisps, as incorporating a social element into group meetings is vital to help with bonding.

The decision to have twenty lessons at each tier was inspired by the 20-letter structure of the *Ogam* alphabet. The age of this alphabet will be discussed in one of the subsequent chapters, but suffice to say for now that at this time of writing there is no concrete archaeological evidence tying them exclusively to pre-Christian Druids. Nor did the alphabet evolve in a hermeneutically sealed Celtic world, for the Latin alphabet significantly influences the structure. The only such Druidic link we have is from the myths, some of which were written down long after general conversion. Such ties do not stand up to academic scrutiny, but thankfully no religion on earth has ever required the approval of a panel of post-graduates in order to find inspiration in some icon or mandala.

Twenty, then, was as good a number as any. Ultimately it means creating 140 lessons, spread out over the course of seven tiers. The realisation of this did cause a few grey hairs, and radically upped the sale of gin locally! At this point it is worth emphasising that we have not written all 140 lessons, though we do have a working blueprint for them. It is quite possible that by the time we get to Lesson 67 I might completely loose the will to live, and throw the whole system aside and replace it with something far less brain-numbing. Indeed, there have been several points during the writing of this book alone when I have seriously thought of hurling the whole system and the laptop along with it out of the nearest window. This book, we hasten to add, only deals with the first tier of those lessons.

The reader might well ask, at this early stage, why we bothered creating such a formalised structure. We could have just gone on meeting, holding a few rituals, discussing matters of general interest, without the need for such formal structure. Right at the start of our group forming, before any ambitious pedagogic ideas had been contemplated, we were drawn to the god Ogmios. We will discuss him in greater depth later, but for now it is enough to say that he is a god of learning, wisdom, eloquence, and teaching. To misquote, for Him the word is mightier than the sword.

As the group evolved, the presence of Ogmios became ever more obvious, both with appearances in visions, rituals, and the type of people he was drawing to us. When discussing study plans, it seemed right and proper that we should learn by a structured method, and reward achievement in due manner.

As previously said, this book represents our first tier of twenty lessons, which we give out to all newcomers. We have no real idea what the medieval (much less earlier) Irish did to mark the transition of a *fili* (poet-seer) from one grade of learning to another. That they would have done something seems quite likely, as people the world over like to have their efforts recognised. Any excuse for a party! We decided that at the end of each tier members would have a ritual in which they could demonstrate their knowledge and skills, and receive the accolade of their peers ~ more on this at the end of the book. If you have one main person in charge of teaching, then this transition will also provide them with a welcome break. Give them a month off to lie down in a dark room with a gin-sodden flannel over their face.

We hope you will find this book enjoyable, if you choose to use it as a teaching aide (or even if you don't). Learning is far easier to acquire if you enjoy yourselves whilst you study. At various points in the chapters you will be encouraged to mull over points and compare experiences ~ always much easier to do over a cup of tea and a slice of cake. Make these lessons a social, friendly experience and you will get so much more from them.

There may be a number of reasons why you are reading this book. Perhaps it was the only thing on the bookstand at the airport; or maybe you have a friend or relative who follows this path and you want to know more; or maybe you are looking for ideas to deepen your own spiritual practice.

If you are the latter, then this book was written primarily for your benefit. You don't have to follow the structure to the letter, but the lessons will make more sense if you read them in sequence and take time at the end of each chapter to reflect on the issues raised before moving to the next chapter. There are also suggestions for practical exercises, and you'll probably get more out of the book if you try them rather than skip over them. Certain points are re-emphasised in two or more chapters, largely because it is expected there will be a time gap between finishing the exercises and discussion point in one chapter before moving to the next. The repetition is there in case you have forgotten what you may have read months earlier, and not because we think you are daft!

In practice, we find that the twenty lessons take about 18-months to cover when working in a group, as they are interspersed with rituals, trips to the woods, days out at sacred sites, and countless breaks for tea and sponge fingers. The lessons have been used with British and American prisoners working in a solitary capacity, and they have taken roughly the same time. The rate at which they can be read and assimilated by someone equipped with this book is uncertain, but just remember it's not a race and you won't win prizes for finishing it first!

Chapter One

A Snapshot of the Early Insular Celts

We cannot discuss the Druids without also exploring the Celts themselves. Who were these tribal peoples who have captured the imaginations of so many people today? A widely held theory, favoured by historians like Dr Anne Ross, holds that, at some point in the distant past, groups of early Celts swept across Europe. They settled in various locales en route before ultimately reaching Britain and Ireland. Their intellectual and priestly caste, the Druids, went with them. When they arrived in Britain they found small native tribes, descendants of the builders of Stonehenge etc, and either killed or intermarried with them. One wave spoke dialects of a language called Goidelic (from which modern Irish, Scots Gaelic and Manx derive), whilst a later wave spoke dialects of Brythonic (from which Welsh, Cornish and Breton stem). Linguists point out the similarities between the two language groups shows a common ancestry, probably evolving separate characteristics when one collection of tribes migrated to Ireland and the other remained behind in Britain.

Alternative theories of British and Irish history, as put forward by historians like Simon James and Barry Cunliffe, allow for migrations across the Continent but suggest a different account for Britain and Ireland. They suggest that Britain and Ireland were not actually invaded by large waves of Continental Celts at all. Rather, the old native Bronze Age tribes simply evolved more and more complex societies. A small number of Celtic traders may have moved here (and native Britons gone over to the Continent), exchanging ideas, technologies, language, and religious/cultural beliefs in the process. However, this was done on a largely friendly basis, rather than as a hostile mass invasion. This theory implies that the British tribes are actually much older than previously suggested. Which of these theories (if either) you choose to believe, is entirely up to you. It is these British and Irish tribes that are often referred to by modern writers as the Insular Celts, to distinguish them from the continental tribes.

Julius Caesar[11], Pliny and a number of other Classical writers, suggested that Britain was the home of the Druids' religion, and that Continental Celts sent their sprogs to Britain in order to learn to be Druids. This has always seemed rather odd, if Britain (as often supposed) was the last place the Celts got to, and therefore the place where Druidry was actually youngest. However, if we suppose that the migration of religious ideas actually went in the opposite direction then it makes a little more sense. This would accord with Pliny's claim that Druidry originated in Britain. It is an intriguing possibility that the Druid religion may have been about the only one to evolve from Britain's soil. In a subsequent chapter we will look in more depth at what Druids were historically, and what they might be today.

It is worth bearing in mind that the tribes of Britain and Ireland never actually called themselves 'Celts', or felt any great loyalty to each other. The word Celt derives from the Greek word *Keltoi*, and was used alongside the term *Galatae* (which means either 'spear-throwers', something that might fail to amuse white supremacists, or perhaps 'fierce') ~ a title favoured by a number of continental tribes. The old tribes were independent political entities, and most likely evolved their own local customs, styles of dress, favoured recipes etc, but were probably united by a common religion. A comparable situation can be seen in medieval Europe, where there were lots of rival nations (French, German, Italian etc.) who were all under the sway of the Roman Catholic Church. The story of Amergin Óg being expected to make a judgement about the divisions of Ireland between his own people (the *Milesians*) and that of the mystical *Tuatha Dé* tribe may suggest that the authors believed that Druids were expected to be free of tribal loyalties. He was warned that if his judgement were unfairly biased towards his blood relatives, he would be killed. The earliest surviving version of the *Lebor* comes from the CE 1150 Book of Leinster, and many may well wonder how accurately a late 12th century monk would understand the role of Druids, most of who had died out about 400 years earlier. It would be lovely to think this story of Amergin does accurately reflect the ambassadorial nature of Druids, but it would be more cautious to say that what it shows us is how 12th century Christians viewed their spiritual predecessors[12].

Given that each tribe was different in subtle ways, it is hard to make broad descriptions that would have been true of all the British tribes. What we do know comes to us partially from the writings of occasionally condescending Greeks and partially from hostile Roman authors (hostile initially because the Gauls invaded Rome in about 390 BCE, later because the Romans themselves were invading Gaul and Britain).

Most Classical writers generally describe the "barbarian tribes" as having a warrior aristocracy, which may well have included warrior-women[13], who ruled over small rural tribes that formed constantly shifting alliances with each other. The religious castes were accredited with considerable social influence, even to the point of being able to make or break kings, start or end wars. These tribes were inclined to such shocking (by Mediterranean standards) behaviours as head hunting, dyeing and spiking their hair into wild styles, heavy drinking and feasting, bragging and boasting, promiscuity and extreme vanity in both sexes. Those parents who now bemoan the odd trends of teenage fashion might reflect that the most conservative pillars of the community once sported the supposedly modern punk look!

Tattoos were popular, such that the Romans called the *Cruithne* tribe "Picts", meaning Painted People. Permanent tattoos are a means of both decoration and communication in various cultures around the world ~ different designs acting like badges to declare such things as social status, tribal alliance, marriage, number of children etc. Temporary tattoos, painted on with woad and other plants, were used like talismans and can impart protection in battle, courage, aid from a particular spirit etc. This is a magical art being rediscovered by followers of Celtic religions today.

They were also expected to be very honourable and, once giving their word, would stick to it. Caesar said he was surprised that the Druids would pile up great mounds of treasure after a battle, as an offering to the Gods ~ but would not leave anyone to guard the treasure, because none of the tribe would even dream of stealing it. Reputation was very important, and affected social standing. Tribesmen wanted to be thought of as courageous, loyal, wise, honest, generous and just. To be regarded as cowardly, tight-fisted or dishonest could lead to a person losing all status, and even being driven out of the tribe.

Most of the commentators describe the British religious caste has having three major subsets, that of Druid, Bard and Ovate ~ called *Druí, Fili* or *Fáith* in Ireland. These are the oldest Gaelic forms of those words, a fact which I contemplated pretending to be clever enough to have known all along, except no one would believe me (all praise goes to Dr Mark Williams for his invaluable linguistic advice, and being kind enough not to batter me to death with the first draft of the manuscript). The Druids served as priests, officiating at religious ceremonies and interceding with the gods on behalf of the tribe. They also served as advisors to kings and powerful aristocrats, giving guidance upon matters of law, morality, politics and general matters of state. Many tales impart to them considerable magical abilities and a great knowledge of medicine, surgery and herbal lore.

The Bards of Wales and *Filid* of Ireland were poets and story-tellers. While this may not sound very impressive, it must be borne in mind that they were in effect walking libraries. They were expected to know vast numbers of myths and religious tales, to remember the histories of the tribes amongst which they lived, to have an in depth knowledge of the genealogies of the monarchs they served. In the days before TV, a Bard could serve as a wonderful PR man, singing the virtues of a chief to all and sundry. By the medieval period the *filid* were expected to know large tracts of legal information. At that stage in history the *Druid* had largely been superseded, and it may be that the law was originally their province.

The 14th century Book of Ballymote describes these *Filid* as having seven grades or ranks. On reaching the highest rank of *Ollamh* the poet was expected to know many hundreds of stories, poems, verse metres, and so on.

The ovate or *fáith* class were regarded as chiefly concerned with divination and prophecy, as exemplified by the role of the lady Fedelm in the *Táin Bó Cúailnge*. The techniques used are varied. Some writers describe them as studying bird flight and the Romans also suggested they studied death spasms[14] for divinatory purposes, and they might also have used the ogam, an alphabet full of symbolism and poetic imagery. A number of myths refer to ogam being used in a magical context. Comparatively little is known of these mystics, though it must be born in mind that divination is fundamentally concerned with understanding the patterns of the Divine, not with fortune-telling at the end of a pier! One need but look at the importance attached to augurs in Ancient Rome or astrologers in modern India to see that this skill is valued tremendously in some societies.

In Ireland there survives a strong body of stories about five great tribes of supernatural beings who held sway before the coming of mortal kind. Most of these clans remain rather shadowy, but one remains particularly prominent in the surviving tales. The *Tuatha Dé Danann*, the People of the Goddess Danu or Anu. They form a sprawling, and frequently brawling, tribe. Amongst their number can be found the extremely popular Bride (also called Brigit), a ferocious warrior woman and patroness of agriculture, healing, poetry and blacksmithing... the gentle swan god Óengus mac Óg, giver of love and romance... and Ogma, patron of the *Filid* and giver of eloquence, poetry and the magical ogam alphabet.

In Welsh lore the magical family are called the Plant Dôn, meaning the Children of the goddess Dôn. There are some parallels to the Irish myth structure, though only a few characters in one match to a character in the other, and sometimes this is more a similarity of name rather than any shared character. If Cornwall or other regions of Britain ever had their own distinct myths, not enough has survived the passage of time to form a comparable body of literature to the Welsh and Irish sources. The Scottish sources are essentially derived from Ireland, though they may well have had many unique tales of their own before the Gaels began to colonise their land.

It is worth pausing a while to reflect on the nature of the literature that has survived. All of those manuscripts known about come from monasteries and were penned by scribes in the employ of those institutions. The monks were essentially recording what they believed (accurately or otherwise) to be the histories of their peoples. Whilst some cultures do regard their own history to be sacred, it is doubtful if the scribes viewed their task as a sacred one or the stories they were recording as myth (in the sense of being sacred tales). The monks may no more have viewed the *Lebor Gabala* and its ilk as sacred than people today would regard a book about the Second World War as holy or mystical. Though perhaps the hagiographies might have been considered devotional works.

To many Pagans today those particular histories which speak of Pagan Gods are considered as mythical or sacred writings, and there is clearly a peculiarity in defining what makes any text sacred ~ the intention of the writer or its reception by the reader.

The function of the histories is also an interesting issue to contemplate. For example, were they intended to be read aloud in what was still a predominantly oral culture? There are certainly some deeply visual passage in some of the manuscripts which, to a storyteller, definitely sound like a script intended for a performance piece. Sections of other manuscripts read more like crib notes, prompts to be fleshed out rather than read straight. The primary purpose of the histories may have been a combination of creating texts that could be used by contemporary and future historians, lawyers etc, and also forging social and political identities that bridged the Pagan past and Christian future.

That history is an important tool in shaping communal and personal identity should not be overlooked. Disputes as to who is descended from which ancestor have not only waged in matters of inheritance or the supposed political validity of noble dynasties, but also strikes to the root of how even the most humble individual defines herself and her place in the world.

The ancient Britons and Irish were polytheists who perceived their deities as unique and individual. They did not see their Gods as all-powerful, but as great spirits whose good will could be won in exchange for honourable service and the performance of rituals. They also believed in many other types of spirit, such as the ancestors and animal spirits. The Patrician writings of a monk called Tírechán might perhaps hint at how the Gods might have been seen. These date back to approximately 670CE, when Pagans were still around in Ireland, so it is not unreasonable to suppose that the scribe may have drawn upon overheard conversations when he put the following words into the mouth of Ethne, Pagan daughter of King Lóegaire:

Who is [your] God and where is God and whose God is he and where is the place he resides? Does your God have sons and daughters, gold and silver? Does he live forever, is he beautiful, is his son fostered by many, are his daughters beloved and beautiful to the people of the world? Is he in the sky or in the earth, or in the water, in the rivers, in the mountains, in the valleys? [...] how is he loved, how is he found? Is it in youth or in old age that he is found?

25

The scribe's implication seems to be that Ethne is comparing the new deity to her old ones, and the qualities that she would associate with them. The passage reads rather like a primer for missionaries, a guide on how to integrate this One God into the traditional perspectives of their targets. The mention of the great outdoors wherein gods might be found may conjure up the popular image of Druids dancing in forest glades. Though they did have wooden temples, Classical commentators often refer to them as meeting outdoors in woodland groves.

The question of whether the new deity is found in youth or old age echoes to such figures as the elderly Cailleach or the youthful Maponos. Just as the early tribes saw their deities in mountains and rivers, so they may have also expected to see them manifesting in their fellow humans ~ with maybe some deities being especially associated with certain types of people (be that on the basis of age group, profession, hair coloration or some other factor).

Over the next nineteen chapters, we will look at what we know of how they performed rituals, what they believed about their Gods, how those spirits can guide us today, matters of morality and ethics etc. We will also reflect on how these old beliefs and practices both influence and can potentially inspire people in the 21st century (or beyond, if ~ miracle of miracles ~ people are still reading this text in a hundred or more years time!)

Some questions for you to think about:

- What are the popular images (good and bad) associated with the Celtic countries and peoples? What feelings do these images evoke for you?
- The land mass now called England was once inhabited by Celtic peoples, yet we no longer think of it as Celtic. Genetic tests have shown that quite a few people who consider themselves English are descendants of the Iron Age tribes. What are the factors that form or challenge both personal and

national identity?

- What makes a person Celtic? Is it being descended from a particular bloodline, or being able to speak one of the languages, or having been raised within a certain culture, or having a spiritual relationship with certain Gods or spirits? Is a combination of two or more of these factors, or something else entirely?

Practical exercise:

Try to find out something about the tribe that occupied the place you live in during the Iron Age. There may be items in local museums to look at, old hill forts you could visit, or books to read about any of the more prominent members of your local tribe. If you are not a European resident, you can still investigate the tribes that once lived in your part of the world. Part of being a Druid involves understanding the land on which you live, regardless of where in the world you are.

You may also wish to reflect on the ways in which the various waves of people have shaped and affected the land on which you live ~ through processes such as deforestation (or reforestation), diverting the courses of rivers, flattening old hills or creating new ones etc.

Chapter Two

Druids Ancient and Modern

The word Druid conjures up all sorts of images. For some, they see old men with Gandalf beards, wearing white robes and dancing round stone circles. Others imagine the same old men spattered in blood as they sacrifice virgins in true Hammer Horror film style. Some imagine tree-hugging mystics communing with nature in a lonely forest glade, whilst others envision upper-class twits engaging in some kind of Celtic Free Masonry. Strangely, few people imagine female Druids as their initial image.

There is no "One True" version of Druidry, as each person finds in it something unique for them. Professor Ronald Hutton has written an excellent book, 'The Druids: A History', looking at the various stereotypes. The ancient Mediterranean world gave us two contrasting images of how they perceived the Druids. In his Annals of CE 78 the Roman writer Tacitus, gave a second-hand description of the attack on the Druid colleges of Anglesey some seventeen years previously, saying:

They deemed it, indeed, a duty to cover their altars with the blood of captives and to consult their deities through human entrails.

This makes the Druids seem quite revolting. However, it is worth bearing in mind that the Roman authorities despised the Druids for stirring up political resistance against the occupation of Britain. The general Suetonius Paulinus was directed to massacre the Druids on Anglesey for this very reason. The evidence for human sacrifice in Britain and Ireland is quite limited, and it may well be that Tacitus exaggerated what did go on in order to justify the actions of the Roman army.

Other writers portrayed the Druids as people of great wisdom and social standing, giving them a more positive image. In 'Lives *of the Philosophers'*, written in CE 230, Diogenes Laertius said:

> *Druids make their pronouncements by means of riddles and myste-*
> *rious sayings, teaching that the Gods must be worshipped, and no*
> *evil done, and manly behaviour maintained.*

Pomponius Mela's *'De Situ Orbis'* of CE 50 went into even more detail when he stated:

> *[The Celts] have, however, their own kind of eloquence, and teachers*
> *of wisdom called Druids. These profess to know the size and shape of*
> *the world, the movements of the heavens and of the stars, and the will*
> *of the Gods. They teach many things to the nobles of Gaul in a course*
> *of instruction lasting as long as twenty years, meeting in secret*
> *either in a cave or secluded dales.*

Some of these more glowing writers came from cultures that actively traded with Celtic tribes, so they might have been laying it on a bit thick in order to curry favour. It certainly isn't good for business if you insult your trading partners! The upshot of this is, the ancient Celts (like every other ancient society) may have done things which modern people would find quite horrible ~ yet they also engaged in many things that would be of great benefit to us now. As modern Druids we look to continue the good, and to understand the reasoning behind the more unpleasant activities (always bearing in mind that many of the things our society does today would have seemed quite awful to our ancestors, and may be roundly condemned by future generations).

In using quotes from Classical sources it is worth bearing in mind that not all writers are considered of equal value. Some lived or travelled amongst the Celtic nations and wrote of what they had witnessed, whilst others repeated second or third hand information.

The Druids themselves did not believe in writing down their

philosophies and rituals. When they were killed during the Roman Invasion, and survivors later censured by some Christian missionaries, much of their knowledge and ideals were lost. It is difficult to say with certainty precisely what the old Druids believed, or how exactly they worshipped. However, we do have some comments from Classical writers that give us lots of clues and pointers. Pomponius again told us:

> *One of their dogmas has come to common knowledge, namely, that souls are eternal and that there is another life in the spirit regions... And it is for this reason too that they burn or bury with their dead, things appropriate to them in life.*

Other writers repeat this notion that the Celts believed in an Afterlife that was similar enough to this life that the dead would require their daily possessions in the Otherworld. Lucan's 'Pharsalia' of 60CE expanded on the Druid view of the Afterlife when he told us:

> *...Rather you tell us that the same spirit has a body again elsewhere, and that death, if what you sing is true, is but the mid-point of long life.*

So we see that after death the Druids felt that people reincarnated into another body of some description, rather than just wafted about twanging a harp on a cloud. Many writers, especially the Greeks, felt that there was much in common between Druid beliefs and the philosophies taught by Pythagoras. Some assumed the Druids had learned from Pythagoras, and others felt the reverse was true. Pythagoras lived in the 6th century before Jesus, and some aspects of his teachings do have a "Celtic feel" about them ~ for example, his view that the human soul had three aspects to it. He also taught reincarnation, particularly a school of thought called Transmigration (which was also attributed to the

Druids) that says a soul can return as any species, not just in human form.

The extent of the similarities to Pythagoras' teachings is difficult to assess, particularly given that nothing in the philosopher's own hand survives. We have accounts of Pythagoras from his disciples and other observers, but it may well be that some commentaries are inaccurate. However, the surviving descriptions of the old man's teachings do have a number of distinct similarities with what we know of Celtic teachings.

Most Greek women were largely disenfranchised in Pythagoras' day, and seldom educated. However, the great thinker's wife Theano foreshadowed Hypatia by writing books of her own on such topics as mathematics and medicine. After Pythagoras' death Theano and their daughters took over running the school. Clearly both Pythagoras and those men who continued to study with Theano had a high, maybe fully egalitarian, view of the female intellect. In CE 275 Vopiscus recounted a tale of how the young Diocletian (in the days before ascending the imperial throne) made daily consultations with a Druidess of the Tungri tribe in Gaul. This echoes the tales of prominent Irish female characters.

Both Pythagoras and the Druids were believed to reject the notion of keeping written records of religious or spiritual matters. Long lists survive of the *akousmata*, the cryptic Zen-like sayings by which Pythagoras taught. The Druids likewise were meant to make great use of obscure sayings, which can also be found in some of the riddling contests between mythic characters such as Diarmuid and Gráinne.

Pythagoras is famed as a mathematician, but it must be born in mind that he also considered numbers to have a metaphysical aspect. We have little direct evidence of this from the Druids, though they appear to have coded much information into Triads. The number-based Bricriu's Ogam, which is a variant form of the

Irish alphabet that has such strong symbolic connotations, could possibly be a remainder of an earlier form of Gaelic numerology.

The Druids held considerable influence within Celtic society. The Greek writer Dio Chrysostom, who put his thoughts to paper around CE 100, seems to be ladling it with a trowel when he claimed that:

...without [the Druids'] advice even kings dared not resolve upon nor execute any plan, so that in truth it was they who ruled, while the kings, who sat on golden thrones, and fared sumptuously in their palaces, became mere ministers of the Druids' will.

The Greek writer Diodorus Siculus, in 8 BCE, gives us an example of an unusual degree of power exerted by these Celtic holy men and women:

Often when the combatants are ranged face to face, and swords are drawn and spears bristling, these men [the Druids] come between the armies and stay the battle, just as wild beasts are sometimes held spellbound. Thus even among the most savage barbarians anger yields to wisdom, and Mars is shamed before the Muses.

The image of Druids putting an end to a battle seems to sit oddly with the idea of them as sadistic old loons engaging in endless gory sacrifice. Whilst people like Tacitus might have seen the Druids as tyrannical monsters, not all Roman citizens saw them in such a bad light. The emperors Diocletian and Aurelian consulted Druids for prophecy, and people like Decimus Ausonius spoke proudly of the fact that their friends were descended from Druids (which also tells us that Druids married and had children). Even amongst the early Christians there were some positive views of Druids.

We also gain information on how the Druids organised themselves from the writings of travelling Greeks and Romans.

Strabo in CE 10, writing of the Gaulish tribes, said:

> ...there are generally three classes to whom special honour is paid ~
> the Bards, Vates and the Druids. The Bards composed and sung odes;
> the Vates attended to the sacrifices and studied nature; while the
> Druids studied nature and moral philosophy. So confident are the
> people in the justice of the Druids that they refer all private and
> public disputes to them...

This concept of there being three types of mystic amongst the
Celts is reinforced by various other sources. Strabo's basic
description of what each did is consistent with other sources.
Julius Caesar, for example, listed the duties of the Druids as
including ~ settling legal disputes, investigating murders, judging
wrangles over land ownership, performing ritual and making
offerings, teaching the children of the tribe, study astronomy, and
communing with the Gods. The word Druid does not crop up in
surviving records from the Galatian Celts however there is
mention of a type of judiciary who may have served the same
function under a different name. Caesar also gave more information on how the Druids of Gaul were organised:

> But one presides over all these Druids, who possesses the supreme
> authority among them. At his death, if any one of the others excels in
> dignity, the same succeeds him: but if several have equal pretensions,
> the president is elected by the votes of the Druids...

Many modern Druid Orders have a leader usually called an Arch-
Druid, or some similar title. It is interesting to see that the ancient
Druids exercised some degree of democracy in the choice of their
leaders, much the same way as the Chieftain of the tribe was voted
for amongst an elite body. What is currently unknown is whether
all Druids in all tribes had the same leader, or if each region had
its own Arch-Druid.

As you can see the ancient Druids were defined not only by what they believed, but also by what they did. It was as much a job description as a religion. It is debatable if a person can really be a Druid if they have no tribe to work for. This doesn't mean that someone cannot follow the same Gods quietly by themselves; just that being a Druid is largely a matter of being able to offer services to friends, family, and the wider community.

Obviously modern Druids can no longer walk on to a battle-field and command the armies to depart in peace. Nor can we be advisers to kings and politicians. Some things have changed beyond our power to reinstate them, which is possibly just as well. However, other duties are still viable. Bards can still compose poetry; praise or condemn through the magic of their words; bring the histories of their people to life. Ovates can still prophecy the future; counsel people; and make offerings to the Gods. Druids can still teach the old ways; give advice on how to live an ethical life; conduct ceremony; heal the sick; study the natural world etc.

Modern interest in Druids began to revive in the 16th century. Iolo Morgannwg published a book called the Barddas, supposedly based on previously unknown manuscripts by a 16th century Welshman named Llewellyn Sion, in 1862. These days most historians think the *Barddas* was a forgery in parts or entirety, but it certainly helped to get people thinking about the Druids. Whilst some class it as forgery, others take a more chari-table view that it was a visionary work and so still worth studying. A lot of the Druid groups in the 16th, 17th and 18th centuries were very concerned with Celtic nationalism, and opposed the dominance of English and French governments. These days many are still actively involved in preserving Celtic languages, ancient sites etc, but party political causes are far less common.

One of the earliest revival groups that formed was the Druid Circle of the Universal Bond, in 1717 (founded by John Toland.)

To put that in a global context, the Sikh faith was founded only eighteen years earlier and is now regarded as a respectable mainstream religion. In 1781 Henry Hurle formed the Ancient Order of Druids. Iolo Morganwg, himself the publisher of supposedly ancient books (subsequently proved to be forgeries), formed the *Gorsedd*, in 1792. Again for global context, the Baha'i Faith wasn't founded until about fifty years later. Most of the groups formed during this period mixed elements of Pagan Druidry with Christian ideas, and concepts from the Eastern religions. Some groups from this period still exist today. Historians often refer to these lodges as Romantic Druids to distinguish them from the Iron Age Druids.

One of the reasons why so many people tend to imagine Druids are all white-robed old men with long beards is due to these Romantic revivalists. Many of them felt that there was a link between Christianity and the Druids ~ some even believed the Celts were descended from the Thirteenth Tribe of Israel, or that Jesus spent time in Britain either during those years which the Bible says virtually nothing about, or after what the Bible presents as his death on the Cross. The common image of a Biblical patriarch is that of a wise old man with a long white beard and a floaty caftan. So when artists illustrated books on Druids, they often drew pictures very similar to the ones found in biblical literature. That and, in keeping with the fashions of the day, many of those revivalist Druids *were* middle-aged and elderly men with long beards.

There are Classical and medieval sources mentioning female mystics, though whether they were actually Druids or some related profession is a matter of contention. Caesar was one of those who thought that it took a good 20 years to train as a Druid, so they might well have been of mature years (though we don't know how young they were when first enrolling at "Druid school"). As to beards... facial hair was popular amongst the Celtic tribes, but mostly in the form of moustaches rather than beards!

Though who knows ~ fashions change constantly. There are Irish and Greek sources to say that Druids wore white robes, but only for certain occasions. They appear to have had different garments for different types of ritual. Whilst on the topic of appearance, the text by Tírechán mentioned in the previous chapter describes a Druid called Máel converting to the Church and shaving off his hair so as to loose his *airbacc giunnæ* ~ a druidic hair style that seems to have involved shaving or cropping the forehead. This may have been something unique to Ireland, or a more widespread practice. Alas nature is giving some of us an *airbacc giunnæ* whether we want it or not! I have yet to encounter a modern Druid who shaved their head in this manner, though some may well have done so.

During the 20th century a growing number of people wanted to learn about what the original Druids believed, and to explore their religion without mixing in unwanted notions from monotheist religions. In the last twenty-odd years a huge number of web sites have sprung up, making previously difficult-to-access information about the earlier cultures readily available. On the downside, along with the previously obscure research has bloomed a vast quantity of total codswallop. Some of it is fairly blatant nonsense that requires no great talent for blagometry[15] to spot. Other examples of misinformation are much harder to detect, because they are either framed in impressive language or are presented by people who have (or claim to have) the kind of qualifications that awe many into submission. Someone at some point has suckered us all in, and the chances are that you, dear reader, will be conned too.

For a brief diversion, this raises issues for the Pagan community in general. The nature of much that we (and, indeed, most other religions) do and believe is intuitive and subjective, therefore difficult to verify with objective evidence. This enables the less-than-honest to claim to have had all manner of experiences, visions and revelations that are hard to refute.

I tried to find some statistics to gain a broader picture, but there appear to be no reliable demographics about modern British Pagans. I can only speculate as to what the educational backgrounds of most Pagans are, whether we are mostly graduates steeped in the techniques of research and critical evaluation, or if most people ceased their studies at GCSE or earlier. Many people can, and do, self-educate (none of the people currently in Clan have degrees in Celtic History or Archaeology, but learn as best they can ~ and make endless silly mistakes, as you may have noticed!). However, without the formal training and access to a university-standard library it can be very difficult to know where to acquire rarefied information, or to know how to assess the reliability of academic research. Many of the better academic texts are shockingly expensive, or accessible via subscription-charging websites that may exclude many of the less financially blessed from accessing such research. A brief trawl across Internet sites shows that apparently large numbers of people are still unsure how to pronounce the names of festivals, let alone anything else.

This is not merely restricted to modern Druids, but equally affects those studying any of the other ancient cultures of the world. There is as likely to be as much nonsense spouted about the Ancient Egyptians or Greeks as about the early Irish or Welsh.

Short of all rushing out and getting degrees, which is hardly practical (despite the government's apparent desire to shovel vast numbers through university on courses of increasingly dubious worth), how is the Pagan community to respond to this vulnerability of its members to being mislead? The time may have come for those Pagans with the necessary academic backgrounds to find ways to disseminate their skills to a wider audience (and perhaps pay off their student loans in the process!). Whilst on the topic of dissemination, it is surprising that linguistically-adept Pagans have yet to cotton on to the market amongst their fellow polytheists who might want to learn to speak Irish, Welsh, Anglo-

Saxon, Ancient Greek or whatever is appropriate to their tradition.

Some modern Pagan Druids belong to large Orders, such as OBOD, whilst others work in small independent Clans or Groves. Some cannot find (or don't wish to be part of) a group, and so operate alone. Our Clan is an example of a small independent group exploring the early polytheist religion of the Druids and drawing inspiration from it to deepen our bonds with the Old Gods.

Some questions for you to think about:

- Can you see any parallels between the way the Romans viewed the Druids and more recent political events?
- The ancient Druids were part of a structured hierarchy, whilst many modern Pagans avoid anything that smacks of hierarchy. What have we gained, and what have we lost, by rejecting such power structures? How do you personally feel about the idea of an organised priesthood?
- Given that we have large gaps in what we know of the ancient Celtic beliefs, many people seek to fill them by looking at other religions ~ Hinduism, Christianity, Taoism, other Pagan religions etc. Is this a wise move? What are the advantages and pitfalls of looking to other creeds? Are there any other ways to try and fill the gaps?

Practical exercise:

Research a particular Druid. This could be one from the pages of ancient history, such as Divitiacus; or one from myth such as Cathbad; or one from relatively recent history such as Dr William Price; or even one that is still living (though it might be wise to draw the line at Getafix!). Having found out as much as you can about their life and what thoughts they may have left to posterity, meditate upon them ~ what sort of person do they feel like, what impact did they have in their own day, what lessons do you draw from them now?

Chapter Three

The Gods and Goddesses

In the modern world we like to divide things up into neat boxes ~ Greek gods in one corner, Norse in another, Chinese in yet another etc. The ancient world was somewhat messier. The Anatolians had a goddess called Akta, whom the Greeks so admired they took to worshipping her, pronouncing the name as Hecate. The Romans were so impressed they built temples to her in Rome. As their empire spread, so temples to Hecate were built in all sorts of countries. Many centuries' later bishops in Britain wrote complaining letters about peasants worshipping Hecate. These days Hecate is worshipped in London, Athens, Paris, New York, and Sydney etc. We call her a Greek goddess, yet she was worshipped before the Greeks knew of her, and these days is honoured by every nationality going, in all nearly parts of the world. In what sense is she exclusively Greek? In what sense can any deity be said to have a nationality? Gods do not require passports.

When we talk about Celtic gods we usually mean ones worshipped by British, Irish or some continental tribes during the Iron Age. However, it is worth bearing in mind that some of those deities were popular elsewhere too. Celtic tribes in what is now Holland worshipped the goddess Nehalennia, but neighbouring Germanic tribes also made offerings to her, as did some Romans. Plus these days people who are not even remotely Celtic by birth perform rituals in honour of Celtic deities.

There are hundreds of statues and altar stones found throughout Celtic lands. Many of the statues have no names, and it is anyone's guess who they represent. Some of the altars have names carved on them ~ certain names appear frequently, others only once. We know that some gods were called by several different names, so it is not always clear if ten different altars are to ten different deities, or to the same god under ten different titles.

This seems a reasonable place to stop (you might want to pour a stiff whisky before reading the next bit) and reflect on that impossible-to-answer question: what is a god? The short answer is: we haven't got a clue! However, ignorance has never stopped a good chance to waffle pointlessly, and shall not do so now. Each age tends to have its own imagery and turns of phrase to discuss such deeply abstract matters in. These days it often tends to be either the surreal language of science fiction, or the even odder realms of psychology.

An analogy[16] that I find useful is that of the ant looking at a gardener. An ant lives about 90 days, and that gardener may have quite easily outlasted 284 generations of ants. To all practical intents that gardener would appear immortal to an ant. Not to mention the fact that the gardener is hundreds of times bigger than the insect and behaves, thinks, and feels in ways that must be utterly incomprehensible (not to say mysterious) to it. Would the bug even comprehend that this immense and towering force is a single being? Those colossal columns may appear to move about independently of each other, rather than seem to be limbs of the same creature. If the little ant did guess that the legs were eventually joined, it might assume that the spade and hoe were also somehow attached to the alien force. Would this vast and seemingly eternal force be a god in the eyes of the ant? There may be beings in the universe (not necessarily aliens from the planet Zod, they could well be native to Earth) that are as far removed from us as we humans are from ants. They may be so long lived and strange and unlike us as to appear to be gods or *sídhe* or some other such thing. This is not to go off on some Von Däniken trip where the gods are all aliens conducting sixth form science projects. Rather it is to consider that humans may not be the only intelligent entities in the either the cosmos at large on upon Earth specifically. There may be other things out there and some of those things may want to talk to us.

Why they should do so is another question. To draw upon a fascinating article by Arlea Anschütz[17], why do humans dote upon cats, or why do we rear and train horses, or do any manner of other things involving non-human creatures? Different gods may have different motivations including affection, curiosity, harnessing a creature that can do something they cannot etc.

Whilst many cultures consider the British love of animals to be very peculiar, there does seem to be a basic human drive to work in symbiosis with other species. Zoology shows that we are not the only species to enjoy associations of this sort, so why not suppose that deities also bond with other types of creature?

A related question for polytheists to consider is whether they consider gods to be a discreet species, or is the term more akin to a job description? If the former, then one might expect to be able to draw up a list of characteristics that distinguish a god from a non-god, in much the same way as a zoologist could distinguish a tiger from a leopard. An entity would either be a deity or not, and claims by someone to have encountered the great god Elvis could then be subject to scrutiny. If the latter, then one might envision a series of duties that a deity is expected to perform, with the possibility that all manner of creatures might find themselves being treated (or actively trying to become) gods to other people.

The Ancient Romans, like the Egyptians, considered that all people had a divine spark[18] that could flower through ritual offerings, self-reflection, great accomplishments and so forth. These "little gods" could grow to become notable demigods, primarily post-mortem though some Emperors and Pharaohs were treated as living gods. The Chinese Taoists hold that the Immortals are transfigured ancestors, and for all we know a similar idea may have prevailed amongst some or all of the Insular Celtic tribes.

The concept of immanent deities present in the material world also raises interesting possibilities. Beekeepers sometimes talk of hives exhibiting a sort of 'group mind'; maybe the collective consciousness of a forest ~ all those trees, shrubs, rocks, rivers, badgers, deer etc ~ coalesces into some kind of group sapience which we humans then envision as a deity (such as Cernunnos) when it impinges upon our own awareness? This, in itself, raises the issue of what is capable of having a consciousness in the first place. Present day science normally favours consciousness as a product of brain activity, and therefore requires a creature to have a brain first (and many scientists seem to feel that only certain creatures with brains have awareness, rather than all those things with brains). Animism surely implies that sentience and sapience are not actually restricted to animals with brains, or even necessarily to things that current science regards as alive in the first place.

Within Clan we tend to take a fairly pragmatic approach, placing the emphasis on having mutually beneficial, fulfilling and enchanting relationships with other aware beings[19] as more important than working out precisely which box those entities fit in[20].

Quite how you conceive of the Gods is entirely up to you; whether as trans-dimensional entities, evolved discarnate souls, group minds, or something else again. It probably goes without saying that whatever you or I think, we are miles off grasping the full picture.

We need to stop and think about how the early British and Irish saw their Gods (and whether or not you share their views.) Many Pagans these days believe that all goddesses are aspects of One Goddess, and likewise with the male gods (this idea is usually called duotheism, or duolatry by academics.) This is a perfectly valid belief, but it is worth knowing that there is no evidence that the ancient British tribes shared it. Rather, the indication is that they were polytheists ~ which means that they believed in loads of gods, goddesses, and other spirits ~ each real and separate, not an aspect of anything. At first you might not think it makes much difference, but it does effect how people relate to their Gods.

If a Druid believes that each god is unique and separate, then she must relate differently to each. So having got on well with Flidhais would not guarantee that she would get on well with the Cailleach (in the same way you have to treat each person as unique ~ just because one doctor is nice to you, doesn't mean they all will be, given that each doctor is a separate person with their own ideas and views). It also means that not all Gods might relate well to each other ~ some chemicals when mixed cause an explosion, and so some Gods might cause mayhem if they both turned up at the same ritual!

Notions of good and evil were not very relevant to the old Druids. They had a strong moral code, which we will look at later, but didn't think in quite the same way as most people do today. The Gods are neither good nor evil, they simply are. If a storm rages and lightning strikes your house, it would be silly to accuse the lightning of being wicked or evil ~ it's simply behaving according to its own nature. Though apparently some bishops think Jehovah floods towns due to his dislike of homosexuality (perish the thought that it's anything to do with foolish councils building on flood plains!). Which does provide a rather entertaining (for some of us) antidote to summer droughts. Donn (Lord of the Dead) does not bring death into the world because he is awful or cruel ~ death is natural, it just happens whether we like it or not.

A polytheist also learns that just because two deities have some things in common, doesn't mean they are the same deity, or identical in other respects. Owen and Rhys might both have the same hair colour, but that doesn't mean they like the same music, have the same hobbies, or eat the same food etc. Nuada and Moccus are both rather war-like, but have little else in common.

Most polytheists do not see the Gods as all-powerful. They have their limits, and must operate within the same universal laws as the rest of us. However, the Gods are more powerful than us mortals, and deserve respect. Our rituals do not summon the Gods to attend ~ if a deity wants to turn up, it will do so without an invite, and if it doesn't want to come... well, it won't matter how many candles we dance around, or how much we chant! The Gods can be praised, but it's up to them if they turn up or not. As well as Gods, there are lots of other spirits that we will learn about in a subsequent chapter. There are some spirits that only seem to appear if specifically invited, but we'll cover them in a future lesson.

As you encounter Gods, you will see that each has their own character and temperament. This shapes how they respond to a request, which in turn is likely to influence who you turn to for help. A lot of Greek mythology books talk in terms of Zeus being the god of thunder, Apollo the god of the sun etc. This is fine up to a point, but it's a bit limiting. Gods have lots of interests, just as humans do. The late great Vincent Price, for example, was most famous for acting in horror movies, but he was also a gourmet cook, an expert on Native American art, an author, a father, a husband (several times over) ~ there was more to him than just one dimension, and the same can be said for all of us. When a Druid considers which deity to approach for help with a problem, they don't just look in a book to see who the goddess of that thing is.

Supposing someone wanted help getting a job. If they approach a teacher, she might give advice on how to study for the best qualifications to get the job. A fashion model might give ideas on the best clothes to wear to look stunning at the interview. The clerk at the local Job Centre might show how to write a really good CV. The local gangster might just threaten to terrorise the interviewer into making the "right" decision. They could all help get the job, but each would have a totally different way of going about it. Whose help you sought would depend on what you felt the most effective approach to be. The Gods are the same, they can all help ~ but in very different ways.

The focus so far has mostly been pragmatic, judiciously sidestepping the question as to what a deity is in the first place. Countless myths from around the world talk of the Gods assuming the shape of animals or wandering beggars, yet few people conceive of them as being bound to one particular physical shape. To a zoologist the notion of a living creature having no physical body is nonsensical. At present the idea of living energy creatures is strictly the product of science fiction, though what is one decade's wild imaginings is the next ones accepted fact. We all know that various animals have senses that pick up on things that our senses cannot, so we accept that there is an abundant array of sensory information out there denied us. The beings we currently describe as gods may one day be more readily definable. Suffice to say for the moment that a great many people throughout history have had experiences of profoundly potent intelligences communicating with them. For the most part these entities are benevolent and intimately involved not just with humanity, but also with many other animals, plants and features of the world around us. To speak of them as supernatural is, then, somewhat misguided ~ for they are very definitely of *this* world.

You can learn about Celtic myths without having to be a polytheist yourself. However, it will help you to know how polytheists think in order to understand the myths, and why rituals are done in certain ways.

The names most of us know the Old Gods by now are the versions of them spoken during the Dark Ages and Medieval periods, when the monks and nuns were writing them down. This is not how they would have been spoken in the Iron Age. Some names are known from altar inscriptions, whilst with others linguists have made educated judgements as to how people would probably have called their Gods in the days before Christianity. Some examples are below ~

Medieval Version	Iron Age Version
Lugh	Lugos
Rhiannon / Morrighan	Rigantona
Fionn / Gwynn	Vindos
Óengus	Oinogustus
Beli	Belinus
Ogma	Ogmios[21]
Boann	Bouvinda
Nuada	Nodens
Goibniu	Gobanos
Brigit	Brigantia
Brân	Brannos
Amaethon	Ambactonos

The early Celts saw their Gods as ancestors, and often claimed to be descended from one or other of them. They were, in essence, family ~ part of the Tribe. Caesar said that the Gaulish tribes claimed descent from a deity that he equated with the Roman god of the dead, Dis Pater. Presumably this was some kind of Gaulish All-Father. In medieval Irish accounts the Dagda is given the title *Ollathair*, which means All-Father (though this is not proof that Caesar was referring to a Gaulish version of the Dagda).

The following deity names are from inscriptions found on statues, altars etc during the Romano-British period. Prior to then the native tribes did not (as far as is currently known) inscribe the sacred names. These names, it must be borne in mind, are often Roman attempts to pronounce local words ~ so they are not always exactly the same as the names which the natives used. There may have been many other Gods whose inscriptions have never been found, and we don't know how many of the names below are just different titles for the same Beings.

Andraste	Goddess of victory, called upon by Boudica during the rebellion who released a hare in order to see how the course of battle would go.
Antenociticus	Three inscriptions dedicated to him were found in a small shrine at Benwell near Newcastle-on-Tyne. He is shown as a youth with what may be the beginnings of antlers or horns on his head.
Arnemetia	Most likely this is a title of Nemetona. Temple found at Buxton near a healing spa (just like Nemetona's shrine at the Bath spa).
Belatucadros	God of war and destruction. His name means: "fair shining one". The Romans equated him with their god Mars. Variant spellings include Belatucader.
Belinus	God of light, and referred to as "The Shining One". He is in charge of the welfare of sheep and cattle. He is paired with the goddess Belisama. They were compared with Apollo and Minerva.
Belisama	Goddess of light and fire, the forge and of crafts. She is paired with the god Belinus (though whether she is his wife, sister, daughter or some other relation is unclear). Associated with healing springs.
Brigantia	Goddess of victory known from inscriptions in Britain. Her name means: "The Exalted One". Thought to be the guardian deity of the Brigantes tribe. Sometimes equated with the goddess Victoria. Portrayed with a mural crown, wings, spear, and shield, usually associated with Minerva. Her consort was the god Bregans.
Callirius	Associated by the Romans with their woodland god Silvanus. A shrine to him was found in Colchester. His name associates him with hazel trees. A stag icon was found in the Colchester pit.

Camulus	Celtic warrior god known in both Britain and Gaul. Known to be important in pre-Roman times, and equated with Mars as Mars Camulos. Camulodunum (Colchester) was named after him. He is associated with images of rams.
Cernunnos	God of fertility, abundance, regeneration and wild animals. Cernunnos means "antlered one". The distributions of images show that Cernunnos (or someone very similar in appearance) was widely worshipped in both Gaul and Britain. The name Cernunnos does not appear on the British statues, but the images are near identical.
Cocidius	"The Red One". Mainly worshipped in Northern and Western Cumbria, and near Hadrian's wall. A god of woodland and hunting, also a god of war sometimes depicted with a shield and spear. At Ebchester there was an inscription to Cocidius Vernostonus, (vern meaning "alder tree"). Sometimes syncretised with the Roman Silvanus, and at other times with Mars. A sanctuary of Cocidius is believed to have been near the Irthing River valley.
Corotiacus	God of battle, an image of him found in the village of Martlesham, Suffolk shows a man on horseback wielding two axes.
Coventina	Goddess of a healing spring at Carrawburgh, near Hadrian's Wall. Coventina is usually portrayed as a maiden, naked and resting on waves. She holds a water lily, and in one depiction is shown in three forms pouring water from a jug. Her name is pronounced "co-vent-eena" rather than "coven-Tina" (she ain't an Essex girl!).
Cunomaglus	The Noble Hound (or possibly Noble Wolf). Associated with Apollo by the Romans, either in

his solar or healing capacities (or maybe both). A temple to him was found at Nettleton.

Deae Matres	The "Mother Goddesses". Usually they are seen as a trinity, and shown holding baskets of fruit, bread, or fish. Linked with sacred springs. Statuary found at Cirencester, Bath, Lincoln, and London.
Dea Nutrix	The "Nursing Mother". Clay figurines show the young goddess seated in a high-backed wicker chair nursing one or two infants.
Epona	Horse goddess whose worship was spread all over the Empire, and even had a Roman feast day of December 18th. Epona was always portrayed riding or alongside a horse, and sometimes with plate full of corn, ears of corn, baskets of fruit, a dog, a goose, and a key.
Maponos	Name means "The Divine Son", with inscriptions from Hadrian's Wall and Chesterholm. He is usually connected to Matrona, the great Mother.
Mogons	Name means "The Great One", and is also spelled Mogonus. Dedications to this god, often paired with Apollo, occur at several fort sites around Hadrian's Wall, including Netherby, Vindolanda, Risingham, and Old Penrith.
Nemetona	Guardian of the sacred places, a statue to her was found in Bath. Her worship was also prevalent in Germany.
Nodens	God of healing sanctuaries, much associated with dogs and hunting. Temples to him were found at Lydney Park (which also has lots of salmon and sea-imagery, suggesting an ocean-link).
Rosmerta	"The Great Provider". Goddess usually found as a companion of Mercury in Britain, Germany, and

	Gaul. She appears on a relief, now housed in the Gloucester Museum, holding a plate over an altar.
Sulis	The patron deity of Bath *(Aquae Sulis)*, she was associated with water, hot springs, and healing. The temple at Bath was dedicated to Sulis Minerva.
Taranis	God of thunder and lightning (*taran* is Welsh for "thunder"), symbolized by a wheel. Known archaeologically in Gaul and Germany, and mentioned by Lucan in his play *Pharsalia*, he is linked to Jupiter in an altar from Chester.
Teutates	Mainly found in Gaul, one inscription to him has been found in Cumberland. His name signifies that he is a general patron and protector of the tribes. This may be a personal name, or a generic title simply meaning 'the god of our people'.
Veteris	A warrior god, whose name is also spelled Vitiris. At least seven versions of the same name are recorded in 54 inscriptions, most from the eastern half of Hadrian's Wall. Some of the altars have boars and snakes carved on them.
Vindos	Whilst the only inscriptions to him have been found in Gaul, linguists link the name to Gwyn and Fionn. There is a strong suggestion that both those figures may have their roots in Vindos or Vindonnus (or a deity with a very similar name, with a shrine in France).

Clearly you could spend a lifetime conducting rituals without even beginning to scratch the surface of who half these gods are. In practice most people feel drawn to a handful of deities, often ones with whom they have a close affinity. Some people also find a deity makes itself known to them in order to convey some lesson about an area of life they have no real affinity with (yet). Keep an open mind and see who makes contact ~ it may not always be the deity you assume would be interested!

To flesh out some of the Gods, and make them more than just names on altars, let us take a brief look at some we have personal experience of within our group ~

Ogmios is the main patron of our small group. In Gaelic a patron is called a *Flaith*, and is someone ~ a deity or another person ~ who looks after you in exchange for offerings or support. The Greek writer Lucian described a picture he had seen in Gaul, where this god was shown as a bald old man with thin golden chains going from his tongue to the ears of lots of happy, smiling followers. However, the very early Celts did not think of their Gods as being human in appearance, but embodied in animals and the forces of nature. In Irish myth Ogma (a name with clear, though not undisputed, relationship to Ogmios[22]) is believed to have invented the alphabet named after him, ogam. He is described as a bard, a poet, and given the title of 'The Honey-Tongued' (or Honey-Mouthed) ~ someone for whom language is terrifically important. His other interests, as described in Irish myths, are wrestling and shot-putting! He was also called *Gríanainech* (Sun Faced) and *Thrénfher* (Strong Man), and is certainly a bright, sunny presence to encounter. He is a god that relishes language, learning and teaching.

Lugus appears in numerous place names around Britain and Europe. His Irish form, Lugh, was described in myth as having a *Fomóiri* mother and a *Tuatha Dé* father. His name means 'light', and in one account he is compared to the radiance spreading across the land from the eastern horizon. In one story he arrived at the gates of the *Tuatha Dé* fortress at Tara, seeking admission. The gatekeepers asked him what skills he could bring to the assembly at Tara, and he began to list his talents. Each time the gatekeepers told him that there was already a god who could perform that skill, until at last he asked if they had one person who could do *all* the things listed. Having no one that talented, they admitted him to Tara and gave him the title of *Samildánach*, which meant 'the equally-all-skilled one'. He led the armies of the *Tuatha Dé* in battle to vanquish the forces of the *Fomori*, and afterwards taught many new skills in peacetime. Two of his most popular gifts to humanity were horse racing and a board game called *fidchell*. The Welsh know him by the name of Lleu, and tell the story of how he married a magical woman made entirely out of flowers. It is worth bearing in mind that some polytheists speculate that Lleu and Lugh may be two totally different entities.

Brigantia had a vast tribe named after her who owned territories covering modern-day Yorkshire. The image of the warrior-goddess Brigantia is still around today, on the back of 50p coins (only these days she is called by her Roman name of Britannia). In Ireland and Scotland she was known as Brighid and considered the special protective goddess (or *Ban-Fhlaith*, female patron) of the province of Leinster. Some polytheists do perceive Brigantia and Brighid as two totally separate entities. When a nun of the name Brigit set up a monastery on the site of an old Pagan temple, the stories of the nun (who eventually became a saint) began to entwine with the stories of the goddess. The Abbess Brigit maintained the old Pagan tradition of keeping a sacred fire burning in a grove, which only women were permitted to enter. Even the bishops could not step foot inside the grove at Kildare. Fire is an important emblem of this goddess, who also looks after the interests of blacksmiths, poets and healers. She is a guardian of farm animals (especially sheep), and it was a popular activity on her feast day to leave out bowls of milk for her creatures to drink. The kinds of domestic chores commonly associated with women in Iron Age Ireland were also seen to be under Brighid's aegis ~ things like churning milk to make butter, spinning, weaving, cooking, running a happy home etc.

These three deities are but the tip of the iceberg, but enough to be thinking about for now. You may well have personal experience of other deities, and this would be an ideal time to pause and reflect on what gods you know and how you perceive them.

Some questions for you to think about:

- How do you see the Gods? Do you feel they are real or symbolic? Are there many separate Gods, or are they all aspects of something else?
- Are there any Celtic gods or goddesses you have read about, with whom you feel a connection?
- Can you see ways in which stories about the Gods might be used to convey moral lessons, ideas about the natural world, and advice on how to live or behave?

Practical exercise:

Pick an Irish, Welsh etc myth and read it aloud to a friend (ideally one with the same interests). Discuss the ideas in the myth, and how you each feel about the themes and events. Which characters appeal to you most, and which least? Pick one of the god-like figures in the tale, and discuss how the story might seem from their viewpoint. Why did they act they way they did? Were there any particular animals, items, images associated with them in the myth? If so, what do you think they mean?

Have a go at creating an image of that character in a medium with which you are comfortable ~ you could write a poem about them, or paint a picture, or model an image in clay, carve something in wood, compose a song about them, embroider a banner etc. Try to think about the story and the character as you work in whatever form of artistic expression you most like.

Chapter Four

The Ancestors and the Living Land

Professor James Lovelock wrote a book in 1979 proposing a new theory, which he called the Gaia Hypothesis. This theory suggested that the planet was not just a lump of inert rock floating in space ~ but a living, self-regulating being. Every living creature was like a cell in the Earth's body.

To many scientists today the Gaia Hypothesis is still a radical, controversial idea. To the polytheist cultures of the ancient world it was a truth that even the slowest-witted peasant lived with. Pagans back then (and many today) would take Professor Lovelock's ideas one step further, to say that the Earth is not just alive, but also thinking. It is appropriate that the theory is named after a Pagan goddess.

For the Celtic tribes the land played a central role in their religion. She was the source of their crops, the fodder for their animals, fed the trees that they built their houses from and so forth. Without the land, human life was not possible. That is still true today, though for many people living in cities it is easy to forget ~ when you can buy any sort of food imported from all over the world, all nice and washed and shrink-wrapped in cling-film, and we see more concrete and plastic than we do wood or stone.

The Gaelic tribes called the earth goddess Danu, Anu or Danand, whilst the Welsh tribes called her Dôn. When a chieftain took office, he symbolically married the land. Bishop Gerald of Wales, writing in the 12th century, described the inauguration of a chieftain in County Donegal. The ritual that he described, in which the chief had sex with a white mare (even allowing that he might have made some of it up), sounds like a ceremonial marriage to the land. The nature of this ceremony has often proved a topic of ribald comment, as you might imagine! The more sensibly minded have raised the 'Health and Safety' concern that a man standing at close quarters to a horse's rear whilst jiggling about is very likely to get a bone-breaking kick. The practicalities of the ritual Gerald described make it seem highly likely that his account was a tad flawed.

The quality of his rule was judged not just in terms of battle victories and political alliances, but also in regards to harvests, animal birth rates and public health. In the *'Testament of Morann'*, which is dated to approximately 700CE, it says:

> *It is through the truth of the ruler that plagues and great lightning strikes are kept from the people.... It is through the truth of the ruler that milk-yields of great cattle are maintained. It is through the truth of the ruler that there is abundance of every high, tall corn.*

If the land gave poor crop yields, if the cattle gave little milk and birthed few young, if plagues or bad weather afflicted the people, then this was all seen as reflecting ill on the chieftain. These environmental happenings were not just random chance or bad luck, they happened for a reason. If the Gods were happy with the chieftain, the land was healthy and the people fared well. If the Gods were displeased, then they withdrew their gifts from the tribe and everyone suffered. This theme persisted into later Arthurian legend, with the story of the Wasteland and the Fisher King.

In addition to the various Gods of the land, each area had its own local spirits that inhabited the forests, lakes, rocks, rivers, caves etc. Some were seen as friendly to humans, others as predatory and dangerous. Houses also had spirits dwelling within them, and people were advised to keep on good terms with their local spirits. The Romans called such entities the *genius loci* (spirit of place). No directly equivalent term survives in the Celtic languages, but there are such beings as the *bocain* ~ little old men who dwell in peoples houses and help or hinder depending on how they are treated. The folklore of Celtic lands is full of odd little practices which people are meant to follow in order to keep the Little People sweet. Putting out bowls of milk is a common practice, but it is considered very unwise to offer items of clothing to house spirits ~ for whatever reason, they take offence and cause mayhem in the home!

In a subsequent chapter we will look at the folklore around some of these different types of spirit ~ both those found around the home, and those found out in the wilds.

In 1925 Alfred Watkins wrote a book called 'The Old Straight Track', which introduced the term ley line. Watkins proposed the idea that there are lines of energy flowing throughout the Earth, and that in ancient times people sensitive to these forces chose to build religious sites on them, to tap the energies. Whilst not every Pagan shares Watkins' beliefs, they are certainly popular. They are also quite similar to ideas commonly held in the Far East and elsewhere.

The early Celts made pilgrimages between holy places, a habit continued into Christian times. Whether the paths they trod were chosen because of some natural presence or energy, or just as matters of convenience, we can only guess at now. It is customary when visiting a shrine or holy place to walk round it clockwise for a certain number of times (traditions vary as to how many times, commonly a multiple of three). This may be a hangover from a ritual to the sun, in which worshippers walked east to west in honour of the solar journey. Spirals and concentric circle patterns appear all over Neolithic monuments ~ possible symbols of the sun. They might also reflect peoples experience of certain forms of land energy moving in a circular pattern ~ and the draw to walk in harmony with the flow of the force being a means of tuning into it. There could, of course, be other much less mystical reasons why people chose to walk round and round.

There are plenty of stories about particular places that exhibit magical powers, that humans can deliberately (or accidentally) become involved with. Welsh myth, for example, tells of a hill in Arberth, sitting upon which could induce visions of wondrous things for the nobility ~ what it did, if anything, for mere peasants is not stated! A prince called Pwyll sat on the hill and saw the beautiful Rhiannon and her horse appear on the road near the mound. Linguists point out that the older version of her name is Rigantona, and there are many (both Pagan and otherwise) who consider the medieval Rhiannon to be an echo of an ancient horse goddess. Pwyll eventually went to meet her at the Court of her father, Hefeydd the Old ~ quite where this was located is unclear, except that it was within travelling distance of Dyfed. There are a number of Irish tales in which hunters were so intent on pursuing a white deer that they accidentally slipped through a gate into the Otherworld. Sometimes Otherworldly beings, such as Fand, journey into our realms.

In the last of the waves of invasions mentioned in the *Lebor Gabála*, the poet Amergin divided Ireland in two. The mortals got to live on the surface, whilst the *Tuatha Dé* lived inside the hills, under the surface of the land. As the stories have been told and retold the distinction between deity and fairy has become very blurred, and many Irish legends also refer to fairies living inside the Hollow Hills. Welsh lore may have had a similar sort of story at some point, because they too have the notion of a World Beneath, where fairies and other spirits live.

The Irish have a fascinating body of stories called the *Dindsenchas*, which are tales of place. Much of them derive from the 12th century Book of Leinster. These stories weaving mythical themes into specific places, with accounts of why a certain hill is an odd shape, how a freshwater spring broke through in that particular place, how a mountain got its name etc. Early Welsh histories also incorporate a great many events tied to specific places, or accounting for their formation.

As said at the beginning of the book, we live in East Anglia. For those unfamiliar with the area, such tribes as the Trinovantes and the Iceni once occupied our particular patch. It is easy to imagine that their storytellers regaled audiences with myths about their sacred land and its particular features. Whatever stories they may have told died with them. If the Romano-British told tales of the *genii loci* of local landscape features, then those in their turn have dwindled into nothing. The Angles and other Heathen tribes came later and left many archaeological remains, but of their stories we have only the late Christian ones whose appeal to a modern Pagan audience is minimal. So, in Clan, we wonder at what body of land-stories may have once existed, that saw and celebrated the spirits of our land. We wonder too at what stories we, and others, could create anew to reinvest the spirit in the Sacred Land.

Many readers may also live in places that have few polytheist stories left, and could perhaps take time to sit atop a hill or beneath a tree, and see what dreams may come. Our land, and maybe yours too, has changed since ancient times. There are parts of East Anglia that were underwater and most likely story-less back in Boudica's day. There are places which were around in her time that have long since fallen into the ocean (look up tales of Dunwich, if you like accounts of sunken towns!) Not only do old places need to retell their stories, but also new places may be awaiting new myths.

The Yellow Book of Lecan, circa 1391, contains a curious story called *'Do Suidigud Tellaig Temra'* (*'The Settling of the Manor of Tara'*). This account relates how the five wisest men of Ireland were asked to settle a matter of land dispute, which they passed to their own foster-father, the ancient Fintan. He recalls the arrival at Tara of a handsome giant, Trefuilngid Tre-eochair, who appeared on the day of the crucifixion bearing stone tablets and a branch of Lebanon wood. The allusion would seem to be that Trefuilngid is a biblical figure, foreshadowing the arrival of Christianity ~ indeed, the story says he was either an angel or the

Christian God himself. The giant stayed at Tara for forty days and nights (a possible implication that Ireland in those days was as much of a wilderness as the desert in which Jesus resisted temptation) and summoned seven of the wisest storytellers from each quarter of Ireland to hear his own version of the history of Ireland[23]. Speaking with what was essentially the proprietorial voice of Mother Church he said,

> *I will establish for you the progression of the stories and chronicles of the hearth of Tara itself with the four quarters of Ireland round about; for I am the truly learned witness who explains to all everything unknown.*

Whilst the giant claimed to be the source of learning, he nonetheless relied upon Fintan to fill in much of the detail. Of particular interest is the attribution of symbolic traits to the provinces, *"knowledge in the west, battle in the north, prosperity in the east, music in the south, kingship in the centre"*.

These qualities are further elaborated in a way that seems to speak of older, pre-Christian traditions. The traits are laid out as follows:

North ~ *Her battles, contentions, hardihood, rough places, strifes, haughtiness, unprofitableness, pride, captures, assaults, hardness, wars, conflicts.*

East ~ *Her prosperity, supplies, bee-hives, contests, feats of arms, householders, nobles, wonders, good custom, good manners, splendour, abundance, dignity, strength, wealth, many arts, accoutrements, many treasures, satin, serge, silks, cloths, green spotted cloth, hospitality.*

South ~ *Her waterfalls, fairs, nobles, reevers, knowledge, subtlety, musicianship, melody, minstrelsy, wisdom, honour, music, learning, teaching, warriorship, fidchell playing, vehemence, fierceness, poetical art, advocacy, modesty, code, retinue, fertility.*

West ~ *Her learning, foundation, teaching, alliance, judgement, chron-*

icles, counsels, stories, histories, science, comeliness, eloquence, beauty, modesty, bounty, abundance, wealth.

Centre ~ *Her kings, stewards, dignity, primacy, stability, establishments, supports, destructions, warriorship, charioteership, soldiery, principality, high-kingship, ollaveship, mead, bounty, ale, renown, great fame, prosperity.*

How these qualities came to be attributed to their respective *coiced* (one of the five provinces) remains a mystery. Fintan set up a standing stone with five ridges to mark the intersection of these political, almost metaphysical powers. It is possible that these various attributions may have had some role to play within ancient Pagan religious or magical practice, though we shall probably never know for sure. Perhaps, for example, if a chieftain were to be seated, then a warrior would stand to the north of him, a poet or musician to the south, and so forth. Thus the human would reflect the geographic. Contemporary polytheists may find inspiration in this five-fold pattern, whether at the simple level of drinking a toast to each point or something far more elaborate.

An additional point to consider is whether this pattern is something unique to Ireland, or reflects a more widespread template. Did the tribes of Britain or Gaul have something comparable? Whilst no obviously supportive evidence comes to mind, it may be that these other peoples outside of Ireland attributed symbolism to the territories to their east, west etc. A good few modern Pagans have attempted to ally this pattern with the elemental structure originating with the Greek philosopher Empedocles, and now tremendously popular with Wiccans and other Circle-casting Pagans. Whilst this is a matter of individual choice, there is something to be said for appreciating each culture within its own right rather than trying to cobble them together like some Frankenstein monster.

A place in which ritual is held is termed a nemeton, which is cognate with the Irish word *nemed*, meaning 'sacred place'. A nemeton can be a clearing in the woods, a cave in the mountains, a cove on a beach, or an indoor site. It doesn't matter how big it is, or what shape it is, so long as it exhibits the right energy. What that energy is, depends largely on the purpose of the ritual. Some places are very conducive to healing; whilst others would be better suited to battle, quiet reflection, or fertility. It is arguable whether the mysterious presence stems purely from the land, from the spirits inhabiting the place, from the residue left by previous humans, or other factors besides. If the ceremony is to honour the sun, the Druid might find somewhere that "feels" sunny; if it is to gain victory in battle then they might opt for a venue with a more militant aura to it.

When choosing a place for ritual, one has to think firstly in practical terms ~ where you can get to, is the place overlooked by nosey neighbours, are there trespassing laws involved etc. Having found a potential venue, one can then turn to view it from a spiritual perspective. Some people are very psychic, and would immediately pick up on whether the place was welcoming, whether it felt "right" for the rite. Not every Pagan has grand psychic visions (in fact, most probably don't), but there are other ways to commune with the place ~ sit and meditate, use divination, ask someone else to check it for you etc.

This process of communion establishes certain things ~ will the spirits inhabiting this place approve of the planned ritual, do they want to join in, would they like any offerings left in exchange, and so forth. If the place is unhappy with the planned ritual, the best course of action is to move and find somewhere that is happy.

A nemeton is often referred to as a sacred place. It's worth stopping a minute and thinking about this. If one place is sacred, then it rather implies that other places aren't, that they're profane in some manner. Lots of people today, Pagan or otherwise, accept the idea that some places are profane, prosaic, spiritually dead etc. There is little evidence that our Celtic ancestors held to this view. For them the whole world was holy, and even the most humdrum of activities could be accompanied by singing hymns, chanting, and ritual. A nemeton is not, as such, more holy than the glade down the track. Rather it is better suited to certain activities, certain types of ritual.

Some places feel frightening and hostile. We may feel that they are haunted ~ either by the dead, or by dangerous nature spirits. Simply because a place is hostile to one person, doesn't mean it might not be quite welcoming to someone else. There may be a reason why it is hostile to the first person specifically, or humans generally. In some religions (including some Pagan ones), such places tend to get automatically exorcised and cleansed. Such an approach is not necessary in Druidry, or even desirable.

To be crude for while, not many people like the smell of shit. There is a reason why shit stinks ~ it's full of bacteria that are harmful to us, so we learn to avoid the smell. Yet shit is not "evil" ~ it rots down, feeds the plants, restores nutrients to the soil. There are places that exude the psychic equivalent of a bad smell. Sometimes it may be because there is a very disturbed spirit trapped there, but it may also be because there is some spirit or process going on there which is dangerous to humans, but important in the grand scheme of things (and so best left alone!).

The upshot of all this waffle is: think carefully when choosing a place to work ritual, and don't assume that all types of ritual can be conducted in the same venue.

Up until quite recently few people travelled to any great extent. The civil partner of one of our members tells how he moved to Stowmarket (a small market town in Suffolk) back in the 70's, and met old men who had never actually left the town ~ not even for a bus ride into neighbouring villages. Up until the Industrial Revolution there were many families who had lived for ten or more generations in the same village. The graveyard was full of their ancestors ~ their ancestral blood and bones literally feeding the earth.

Whilst some ancient Celts became sailors and merchants and

mercenaries, travelling as far a-field as Egypt, plenty more lived as farmers and seldom travelled further than the nearest market-place. In Chapter One we mentioned the theory advanced by historians like Simon James, that the Irish and British Iron Age tribes were descended from the Bronze Age natives and earlier. If that is the case, there may have been many villages built a short walk from a Neolithic burial mound containing the bones of their far distant ancestors.

Since childhood one of our members reckons he must have moved house over a dozen times. Like most people these days, he has no real sense of roots. He does not live in the same house his parents did, cannot point to a tree and know that his great-grand-father planted it, or see a hill and know his great-great-grand-mother was married atop it. Knowing that past generations of your bloodline have lived in a place gives a unique sense of belonging to the land, being somehow part of it.

The stories of the waves of invasions in Ireland often have a death take place early on. It may have been an echo of some land-bonding ritual, the sense that the newcomers could take possession of a territory by planting their ancestors in the soil. Some have argued that such rituals may have been enacted with a gruesome sacrifice when people moved to a brand new area ~ interring someone specially bumped off for the purpose of creating a bond. We cannot say for certain that this never happened, though equally we can say that there is no evidence to suggest this happened on a regular or widespread basis amongst the Celts. However, it is worth noting that numerous buildings dating from the last fifteen hundred years have been found with mummified animals under the foundations, under church altars, sealed inside wall cavities etc. Whether these creatures were killed specifically for the purpose, or whether advantage was merely taken of a coincidental death is hard to say. One of our members has buried a fox, found dead at the roadside, under his garden altar. Perhaps in a thousand years time some archaeologist will envision a bizarre rite in which crazed drivers, as part of sacrificial practices, mowed down foxes?

The spirits of the dead have a strong role to play in nearly all tribal religions. It is commonly held that blood ancestors maintain a general interest in the welfare of their descendants. In the Iron Age the Celtic tribes were headhunters, and collected the severed heads of their fallen enemies. They also seemed to have the habit (at least, some tribes did) of keeping the skulls of revered leaders, who may well have died quite peacefully. The most famous legend featuring this sort of incident is the Welsh story of Brân the Blessed. His sister, Branwen, married an Irish chief who abused her. When her brother found out, he led an army into Ireland to punish the chief and his tribe. At the climax of a massive battle, Brân was wounded and asked his war band to chop off his head. The body died, but the head continued to live and talk. For eighty years it entertained and advised the war band.

A number of Classical accounts mention Celts keeping skulls or preserved heads around the house, and bringing them out as talking points ~ much the way people bring out their holiday photos or sporting trophies these days. Some even made drinking cups out of skulls. It was believed that the soul dwelt in the head and, through various magical rituals, a skull could be used like an oracle ~ a medium through which the dead could be communicated with.

People might commune with the dead to seek advice, to be reassured that the loved one is happy in the Afterlife, to gain protection or other forms of help, or just to update them on the latest family happenings. Whilst séances are often (mistakenly) imagined to be rather gloomy affairs these days, many cultures make a great party out of holy days dedicated to the dead. They go and have picnics in graveyards, tell their deceased relatives all the family gossip, recite poems or engage in activities they think the relative would have enjoyed in life.

Tribal chieftains in Britain and Ireland employed poets and storytellers to memorise their family trees, going back nine generations or beyond. These trees could then be recited at important occasions ~ especially if one of their ancestors was famous, and could be bragged about at great length. Many claimed to be descended from certain Gods, and the line between a deity and an ancestor is frequently blurred.

Just as some ancestors are worth bragging about, others might be a cause for embarrassment. It is worth stopping a minute and reflecting on what death is ~ a transition. It is a learning experience, like any. Some people might learn a huge amount from it, whilst others might change very little. A person who was sadistic, avaricious, stupid, boring or bone idle in life might not be that much different after death. It would be unwise to assume that every ancestor is going to be lovely, sweet and wise. If they gave bad advice in life, they might be just as daft in death. So when communing with the dead remember to retain your own judgement and don't feel you have to do absolutely everything some passing spirit tells you to.

In addition to blood relations, there are also many spirits who take an interest in the living because of some shared passion. A great musician might be drawn to still-living musicians. Some of these spirits may hang around for the rest of your life, whilst others may pop in only briefly.

Most polytheist Druids will invite the spirits of their (benevolent) ancestors to join them for rituals. Every year there is the feast of Samhain, at which special attention is given to the dead ~ especially the recent losses. This festival is a good time not only for honouring dead friends and relatives, but also those people who (even if you never met them in the flesh) inspired or uplifted your life in some way... a favourite actor or singer, a writer, an inventor, a great historical figure etc. In a subsequent chapter we will discuss what lies beyond the grave.

Some questions for you to think about:

- What means would you feel comfortable using to try and sense the will of the spirit of a place?
- How far back can you trace your family tree? How much do you know about the lives of your grandparents, great-aunts, long-dead cousins etc?
- How do you view humanity's relationship to the land? Are we its masters, its guardians, just one species amongst many, or something else again?

Practical exercise:

Try to meditate and make contact with the spirit of your house. If possible, ask it what its name is. See if it manifests in a particular way ~ does it look human, animal, or something else? Do you sense any particular aroma, sound, taste etc linked with it?

Having made contact, create a small shrine to it somewhere in your house. Ask what the spirit would like on the shrine, and if it has a preference for any particular type of offering ~ a certain food or drink, for example.

Additionally, consider creating an ancestral shrine with photographs or other mementos of deceased loved ones or much admired heroes. It is a common practice in many cultures to have bowls or cups with food and drink offerings for the Dead, normally of whatever their favourite comestible was in life (this can include things like cigarettes and such like too.)

Create a wildlife area in your garden, a refuge for bees and butterflies, bats and wild flowers. If you live in a flat and have no garden, there may be local conservation schemes that you could assist with (if you don't already). How better to meet the soul of the Land than by getting up to your elbows in it?

Chapter Five

The Sídhe and other spirits

In previous chapters we have discussed the Gods and the spirits of the dead. There are also other entities to think about with Celtic mythology. One of the most important groups of these is the *Sídhe*. Some books translate this word as meaning fairy, but that tends to conjure up images from Victorian paintings of little whimsical Tinkerbell things flitting about with butterfly wings. The *Sídhe* are not cute or whimsical. They are powerful Beings who inhabit the natural world, and who are not always friendly to humankind. Celtic myths refer to the *Sídhe* as large, brilliant creatures with skills and life spans beyond those of mortals.

It seems probable that the word *Sídhe* originally referred to the burial mounds from the Bronze and Neolithic periods, which were viewed as the homes of various Gods and other spirits. In time the word was used not just for the mounds, but also for the various beings that lived in them. The word can also mean profound peace, and has echoes of the Lithuanian concept of *darna* ~ spiritual vibrancy comes from being in harmony (or perhaps accepting) ones own nature; being in harmony with ones tribe, family or wider community; from being in harmony with ones ancestral line and their expectations (recalling the link between the burial mounds and the creatures dwelling within them); from being in harmony with ones Gods and the forces of the cosmos. Peace here does not mean just sitting quietly, but a deep sense of balance, harmony, belonging, and solace.

Sometimes the distinction between a god and a *Sídhe* is blurred, and there are certainly local spirits who have been reverenced and treated in a god-like manner. The spirit tied to a given river may well take on god-like proportions if ones entire family depended on that river for fresh water, food etc. For someone else just passing the river on a day trip, then the spirit is nothing more than "just" a local land wight. This fuzziness is not really a problem, and it's worth noting that Celtic religion probably had little appeal to anally retentive minds that wanted everything nice and neat and pigeonholed.

The *Sídhe* live in the Otherworld, but often journey into this one via portals such as burial mounds or particular trees. Portals are often two-way affairs, reminiscent of the kind of inter-dimensional gateways beloved of so many science fiction films and TV shows today. In the Otherworld they have their own dogs, cats, cattle etc. It is described as very much a sensual, physical place, rather than some abstract world of ethereal harp twanging. These strange creatures can sometimes be seen in this world, and are most commonly identified by their colouring ~ the body is mostly white, but with red extremities (such as ears and paws.) The canine *cu-sídhe* (*cŵn Annwn* in Welsh) was often described as running with hunting parties across stormy skies.

Some readers may ask why such astounding beings, if they exist at all, would bother interacting with humanity. There could be various reasons, including the fact that humanity is now so pervasive as to be hard to avoid. I was struck by a conversation overheard in a pub some years ago, between two gentlemen with alarming beer guts. The younger of the two was raving about some possible UFO sighting, whereupon the bearded one asked laconically why any species so vastly clever as to develop inter-galactic spaceships would waste their time visiting gormless teenagers on Earth. After a pregnant pause and much beer-swilling, the younger responded by pointing out that European cultures sophisticated enough to build large sailing vessels had once visited tribes in the South Seas that still had Stone Age technologies. The question as to why marvellous and magical beings would bother talking to people with bad perms called Maureen[24] is often asked, and one can but postulate that there may be all sorts of reasons for them being spotted to which the human sighting them could be incidental.

In Scottish folklore the fairy people are divided into two courts, each with their own leaders, war bands and so forth. The Seelie Court consists of those beings that are friendly to humankind, and a meeting with the Seelies is usually a positive experience. The hostile, aggressive spirits belong to the Unseelie Court. The savage inhabitants of the Unseelie Court are rather like the Irish *Fomóiri*, mentioned later.

One sort of *Sídhe* that gets frequent mention even into quite recent folklore is the *corpàn-sídhe*, or changeling. Legend has it that sometimes the fairies steal human children (quite why is never entirely clear) and replace them with one of their own, a changeling. These babies look a little odd and frequently act in strange ways ~ screaming incessantly, or eating everything in sight. Folklore gives a variety of ways to encourage the fairies to bring the human child back, none of which are very pleasant. Some folklorists feel that stories of the changeling may have been a way to explain unusual-looking infants ~ ones that had conditions such as what we would call Downs Syndrome today.

It may be worth pausing a while here to reflect on what exactly you consider the function of fairy stories to be. Are they just metaphors and moral tales for children, or are they describing an actual race of creatures? Science fiction has already been mentioned, and a fair few mythographers have noted the comparison between medieval tales of people being taken by the fairies and 20th century accounts of alien abduction. These days many people find it easier to think about creatures from another planet than to consider that there may be other sapient creatures from this planet, but perhaps ones existing at some other level of reality not easily perceived by our standard five senses. One century's Otherworld is another century's Parallel Dimension. Whatever the jargon and conceptualisation, the basic idea is of a world that runs alongside, and often overlaps with, this one. It is certainly not compulsory that one 'has' to believe in fairies to adhere to the larger principles of polytheist Druidry, however they are mentioned a great deal and it is useful to file them somewhere in your mental schema. It is always useful to have a rough idea of where the bounds of your reality lay, what you consider plausible and what ludicrous.

In addition to the shining and radiant *Sídhe*, there are whole ranges of other spirits that do not readily fit into categories. Let us start with a few of the grimmer ones, and then finish on a jollier note. In Irish myth there is a race of entities called the *Fomóiri*, sometimes also referred to as the *Tuatha Dé Domnann* (the Tribes of the goddess Domnu, whose name suggests a connection to the depths of the ocean). Most of the time they are portrayed as hideous, ill-tempered things prone to abusing all they encounter. Some modern books talk of them being evil, and contrast them against the goodness of the *Tuatha Dé Danann* gods. We find this approach unhelpful. Whilst ethics were important to the old tribes, notions of good and evil were largely an introduction by Christian missionaries. The spirits don't fall neatly into boxes labelled "cuddly" and "gruesome".

If a wolf eats a goat, is it evil? To the goat's mother the wolf is a monster, but to the passer-by it is just a carnivore doing what carnivores were designed to do. It would be silly to say a predatory animal is either good or evil; it is simply doing what it must to survive. If a person contracts a virus and dies, is the virus evil? Again, whilst the victim may feel it is at the time they're dying, it would be daft to impart morality to a germ.

For many centuries humans have been the dominant species in Europe. We long ago wiped out virtually all rival predators. We are not used to being viewed as dinner, and the prospect is quite disconcerting. Maybe that is why so many horror films show humans being knocked off the top of the food chain by vampires, werewolves, aliens etc. Included under the label of *Fomóiri* are a number of spirits who (in our experience) just seem to view humans as either totally irrelevant, or as lunch ~ a source of energy that can be battened on and drained. The fact that such spirits might cause us harm does not make them wicked any more than a shark chewing on a swimmer. Sharks have their own beauty, though a wise man observes it best through a reinforced plate glass window at an aquarium. Likewise, it may be safer to view many *Fomóiri* from a great distance.

This is not to say that there are no spirits prone to malicious, sadistic behaviour ~ just that it is too easy to demonise anything that seems a threat to us.

Most myths describe the *Fomóiri* as quite ugly (there is a tendency in Celtic myth to associate physical perfection with moral perfection, which is seldom a wise thing to do). Yet it is worth bearing in mind that both handsome Lugh and Bres the Beautiful were said to be half- *Fomóiri* and half-*Tuatha Dé Danann*. There are also members of the *Tuatha Dé* who cause as much, if not more, destruction than the *Fomóiri* do. As ever, things are more complicated than many books present them as being.

There are also hordes of little sprites that are told of in folklore from around the Celtic countries. A number of statues from the Iron Age depict a central deity flanked by small figures wearing cloaks and hoods, called *genii cucullati*. These may be depictions of Druids or worshippers, or perhaps of local land spirits that acted as messengers of the main deity. Scottish folklore speaks of the *bocanach* or *bodach*, words that mean an old man (especially a grumpy one) and also a small sort of goblin that lives in the house. If treated well they look after the home, but if offended they wreak havoc. Part of treating them well involves talking to them and leaving them offerings of their favourite food or drink. There are numerous stories that say these house sprites are naked, but take offence if ever offered clothing. No one seems entirely sure why this should be so!

House spirits do not just inhabit Scottish crofts or Hampshire semi-detacheds, but any kind of structure. The use a building is put to may well determine the type of spirit that feels comfortable living there. A library is likely to attract a quiet, contemplative soul whilst a nightclub might be full of little raver sprites. There are lots of anecdotes about Pagans visiting homes and encountering house sprites who loathe their new human "tenants" because of the way they act ~ and they often try to drive them out by breaking things, hiding keys, causing electrical malfunctions etc.

Russian and Roman Pagans felt that there were different spirits in each part of the house ~ one sort living in the bathhouse, another in the barn, another in the pantry, yet more in the bedroom etc. Possibly some similar view may have been common amongst the Insular tribes of the Iron Age, we are unlikely to ever know for sure.

Other types of spirit, more often found in the countryside, include the usually gentle *ceasg*, mentioned in Scottish lore, which is rather like a mermaid but has the tail of a salmon and lives in freshwater lakes. These sea-creatures were thought to sometimes mate with mortal men, usually sailors and their offspring showed remarkable navigational skills. *Ceasg* are said to grant wishes to those who can capture or cajole them, and were believed to preserve their souls in separate objects whose possession is often a key factor in the legends told of these aquatic beings.

The *Gille Dhu* lives in forests, dressing in mosses and leafs. Friendly enough, it occasionally looks after lost travellers, and will also help those who are friends to the trees and beasts of the woods. One tale is told of such a being looking after a lost child, and the empathy she felt for it ever after. It is similar to, if not indeed the same as, the Russian *leshi*.

The Welsh *bwca* is probably one of the most famous of Celtic spirits, and entered English folklore under the name of Puck or *pooka*. These spirits change shape a great deal, and few (if any) know what they really look like. Sometimes in the form of a pony, sometimes a goat, one even starred in an old film with James Stewart and took the guise of a giant rabbit! By turns mischievous and dangerous, the *bwca* is a sprite to be reckoned with.

All countries have stories of sprites that inhabit lakes, mountains, woods etc and will be friendly to humans if they and their realm are treated well. Those same countries have accounts of grim and dangerous entities that are no friend to humankind. In some countries this belief remains very strong ~ in Iceland, for example, some boulders are said to be inhabited by elves, and road builders will commonly make a bend in the road to go round the boulder rather than risk offending by removing the rock.

From reading this it may sound as if we are knee-deep in spirits... and perhaps we are! However, there may well be places that have no spirits. This could be because the spirits that were there have upped and left, been exorcised or driven out in someway, or may have died (or whatever it is that finally happens to sprites). Or perhaps because a place is too new to have attracted interest, some Pagans who move into brand new houses say they feel "empty". It may well be that houses, hospitals, libraries and other buildings only attract *bocain* over the course of time.

Some questions for you to think about:
- Do you think these spirits exist, or are they just old stories told by people to explain natural events?
- Do you think house spirits are entities that lived in an area before the house was built, or only migrated there afterwards because they liked the house (or people in it)? Do you have any ideas why house spirits are often perceived as being naked?
- Have you ever seen, heard or otherwise experienced something that might have been a nature spirit? Is it possible that some places, perhaps through pollution or terrible events happening there, might be totally bereft of any spirit presence at all? Have you ever been to a place that felt totally dead?

Practical exercise:

If you have not already done so, try and make contact with whatever spirit dwells in your local river, lake or other body of fresh water. Through meditation, divination or whichever other techniques you prefer, try and get a name for the watery creature, and a sense of its temperament. Try leaving it a gift of food or drink to establish friendly relations. You might want to consider creating a small altar exclusively for his, her or its use (avoid the mistake of automatically assuming all water spirits are female in manifestation).

If your local water source is heavily polluted, full of chemicals and human waste ~ it may be taken as a friendly gesture if you spend an hour or three cleaning up a stretch of it (take suitable safety precautions so you don't turn yourself into an accidental offering!)

It never hurts to research beforehand. Find out if this is an ancient river, or a manmade one. Does it follow its original course, or has it been diverted? What names has it been known as over time? What is its history of use ~ was it ever used for fishing, as a transport canal etc. Where does the river (or lake, stream etc) originate? You could always visit the springs that feed into it. Does this body of water supply your household, or does the stuff that gushes out of your taps come from elsewhere?

Of course, if you think river spirits are just metaphors, then this exercise may seem a tad pointless! However, give it a try with an open mind and see what happens.

Chapter Six

The Structure of Early Gaelic Society

The main focus of this chapter is on Irish society, largely because the records are better and go back to a period when Pagans and Christians co-existed. The records of Welsh society date back to a time when Christianity was pretty much dominant, and the Romans had long-since slaughtered the Druids. In looking at Welsh records trying to pick out native Pagan elements from Christian, Roman, Saxon and (in due course) Norman influences is a lot harder. To some extent this lesson is a bit of historical indulgence, though it may provide inspiration on alternate ways of running society.

The tribes of Britain and Ireland lived a largely rural life up until the coming of Rome. The Romans built the first cities on these shores ~ up until then even the largest settlement hadn't been much more than a village. As with any kind of small-scale life, people would have known everyone in their community by name. They would have depended on each other for survival.

A variety of legal tracts, known collectively as the Brehon Laws, have survived describing tribal life in Dark Age Ireland. It bears a remarkable similarity to some of the things described about Continental Celts by Greek and Roman writers several centuries earlier ~ suggesting that change was a very gradual process.

What comes across is a picture of a caste system in which most of the power was split between the religious caste and the landed gentry (much the same as it was in Europe up until the rise of international corporations).

Everyone was part of a family, called a *fine*. This would consist of several generations, and include aunts, cousins, grandparents etc. The leader of the family was the *cenn-fine*. This man, or occasionally woman, acted as representative for their kinfolk in the law-courts. If a member of the family wanted to make a legal contract ~ such as a marriage, a business deal, buying or selling land ~ then they needed the consent of the *cenn-fine*. If they entered into contracts sneakily, then the *cenn-fine* could revoke them. Think of the *cenn* as rather like the head of a Mafia clan!

The Old Irish word *cenn* (*pen* in Welsh) means both head of the body, but also head of the tribe. Just as the head of a body was seen as the focus of spiritual powers, so the head of a tribe was also a wellspring of magical energies. This is in many ways similar to the role of the paterfamilias in early Roman society, whose soul (the *genius paterfamilias*) was prayed to, that it should guide and inspire the familial head to look after his kinfolk well.

The Celtic class system had two major divisions. The *nemed* were the blessed ones, people considered to have a magical quality to them. Mainly this consisted of the chieftains and the Druids (in later centuries Christian abbots and bishops too). Even into medieval times it was widely believed that European kings had special magical powers, even to the point of imagining that the touch of a monarch could heal disease... though the evidence that it ever worked is scant! The *doer-nemed* were the ordinary people ~ farmers, warriors, merchants, servants, craftsmen etc.

Tribal leaders were appointed to office by a limited form of democracy, in which a group of powerful families would select one of their own number to act as chieftain. This group was known as the *derbhfine*. The person selected was probably most often male, but there are a fair number of references to female leaders in historical and mythical accounts. In addition to choosing a chief, the elite families would also appoint a sort of understudy called a *tánaiste*. If the chief fell ill, was killed, deposed etc, then the *tánaiste* would take over from him, at least temporarily.

History leaves us accounts of the *tarbh-feis* ceremony, whereby Druids used divination and visions to confirm that the Gods approved of the candidate for leadership. In the tale of the *Lia Fáil*, the would-be chief must stand upon an ancient rock and, if he were righteous, the rock would cry out. A deafening silence was scarcely a good omen. Whilst the *Lia Fáil* was brought from another world, modern scholars see it as a metaphor for the land itself. A good chieftain was known not just by his (or her) political decisions and battle victories, but also by the state of the land and the creatures that dwelt upon it. The *'Testament of Morann'* says that:

> *through the Truth of the ruler that milk yields of great cattle are maintained... abundance of every high, tall corn... fish swim in the streams.*

A poor chief, no matter how apparently astute he might have been at politics, was stained by famine, plague, barren cattle and childless women. The Land was, in many was, the ultimate judge of a chieftain's quality. We might consider the state of our own Land and what this says about the quality of contemporary leadership!

The power of a chieftain was maintained through a series of feudal allegiances. To class as a *flaith* or Lord, a landowner must have a minimum of ten small farmers as his *céile* (clients). Should he loose too many clients through war, plague or desertion to a better *flaith*, then he lost all the social status and legal authority that went with his title.

Once a year a chief held a ceremony known as *tuarasdal*, where he expressed his gratitude to his loyal *céile* and famed champions by making them gifts (such as cattle, land, weapons, jewels etc.). One might compare the modern Christmas gift giving as a sort of equivalent, in which people (perhaps secretly, whilst outwardly claiming it's the thought that counts) assess how much someone else values them. In modern Gaelic *tuarasdal* has come to mean a wage packet. The duties of a *céile* were various. They included paying rent on arable or grazing land, raising warriors in times of conflict, and *coinmed* ~ hosting the *flaith* (and his hungry entourage) during tours of the provinces.

The old name for a client-lord relationship was *lánamnas*, which extended to any sort of relationship in which one party had more power than the other, e.g. parent-child, teacher-student etc. In time the term *lánamnas* came to be applied almost exclusively to marriage (in a future lesson you will see that the nine types of Irish marriage were largely based on which partner was the richer). These levels of patronage formed the basis of society at least until the arrival of the Normans in Ireland. A farmer or artisan might be client to a local *flaith*, who in turn was client to a grander chief, who in his turn... and so on up the pecking order.

The relationship between a lord and client may be seen reflected in religious terms. At the human level, an abbess acted as *ban-fhlaith* (Lady) to her nuns and monks ~ and we may reasonably suppose that in Pagan times a high-ranking Druid acted as *flaith* to less experienced Druids. Yet a person might also form the same type of relationship to a god or other spirit. The deity offers protection, healing, advice, knowledge, material goodies etc, in exchange for services from mortal devotees.

Whatever it is that Gods need, one of the important features of *lánamnas* is balance. A lord must fulfil his duties to the client as surely as the client must aid their lord. Parents have duties to children, but in Gaelic law the child (particularly once grown up) also had officially recognised duties to the parent. One-sided relationships were seen as unhealthy. A person who always gives is a doormat, no matter how well intentioned their desire to help. A person who constantly takes and demands is a parasite. Each partner in a *lánamnain* must recognise that they have a duty to give certain things to the other person, but also a duty to allow that person to give back to them ~ there is no honour in emasculating someone, nor in allowing yourself to be rendered servile.

This applies as much to the Gods as to other humans. Hosting a ritual for a god may be seen as fulfilling the *coinmed*, but there should also be expectation back of the deity. If your life is barren, then maybe you need a better head to guide you (either that, or you're not fulfilling your duties to them).

Celtic society operated on a caste basis, where social class was tremendously important. We have just talked a little about the landed gentry, from whom the chieftains were drawn. It should be borne in mind that most of these aristocrats were expected to be warriors and fight in battle, male and female alike. In a previous lesson we discussed the religious caste ~ the *druí*, *filid* and *fáith*. Whilst the Druids (and later Christian clergy) were theoretically the next class down from the aristocracy, in many practical respects they wielded far more power. In the etiquette of the royal court, the Druid had the right to speak even before the chieftain did.

Below the religious caste came what we might think of as the minor gentry ~ farmers of means who owned no land of their own, but rented from an aristocrat. In some respects they were like the cattle barons of Texas, in that their wealth was measured mostly in terms of cowherds. There were various titles, depending on wealth, such as one called the *bóaire*, which means a cattle-chief.

Under the rich farmers were the artisans and craftspeople ~ the carpenters, blacksmiths, furriers, potters, weavers etc. Some very skilled craftsmen could achieve a high rank on a par with bishops and brehons.

Beneath them was a caste that consisted of labourers and servants in the employ of the upper classes, and who rented what land they had off a patron. This system of landlords and tenants changed little over the centuries.

At the bottom of the heap were the un-free. A number of people fit into this category, but the main one was the *fuidhir*. Some books call these slaves, but they were not really slaves in the sense that we mean these days. A better translation would be bondsman. There were a class of people even lower down the pecking order that existed in an exploited state, the men called *mu* and the women called *cumall*.

The early Celts did not have prisons, and they rarely executed or flogged people. Instead making the criminal pay compensation to their victim punished most crimes. If the criminal didn't have enough money, then he lost all his social status and became a *fuidhir* and had his labour contract sold to the highest bidder (the money going to the victim). The buyer could put the *fuidhir* to doing whatever work they felt like ~ most likely all the crappy jobs that no one else wanted to do. They were paid a pittance for this, but still had a few rights in law and could farm a scrap of land. If they could raise enough money, eventually they could buy their freedom. If trusted, they were even allowed to carry weapons. The child of a *fuidhir* was also born to that lowly state, but the grandchild was born free regardless of how much or how little money the family had saved up.

Most people were born to the social status of their father (though in some tribes it may have been the mother's status ~ there is some evidence of this), but could change their class by such means as getting rich, training to become a Druid or Christian cleric, or losing their money and falling down the social ladder.

As well as class, tribe played a big factor in Celtic society. Early Irish law distinguished between two types of people ~ *aurrad* and *deorrad*. An *aurrad* was a citizen of the tribe with full rights in law. The members of a tribe to which your tribe were allied were also *aurrad*, and could travel into your territory and expect to be treated properly.

A *deorrad* was someone with no rights at all. This could be a total stranger from some tribe with which you were at war, who had foolishly wandered into your territory. Or it could be someone who had committed such a horrible crime that they had been exiled from the tribe. Such a person had no rights at all. If they strayed into your tribe land, then they could be attacked with impunity.

It may well have been the case that people sported some means of easily determining which tribe they belonged to at a glance ~ other tribal cultures from around the world use things like tattoos, unique hair styles, and specially patterned clothing (such as tartans) to proclaim their allegiances. Foreign writers commented upon tattoos, unusual hairstyles and such ~ but no surviving accounts tell us the actual significance of these things to the Celts themselves.

Some questions for you to think about:

- What do you imagine it would be like living as part of a strongly regulated Clan ~ happy or too restrictive?
- Is it right to judge people according to their social class? Should everyone have an equal say in society, or should power be the privilege of a few? If power were to be restricted, should the deciding factor be wealth, birth, education, spiritual attainment or some other factor?
- Are there any aspects of ancient Celtic society that would benefit the modern world? What aspects do you think we are better off without?

Practical exercise:

If you have access to a camera, get someone to take a photograph of you. Failing that, study your image in a full-length mirror. Try to objectively assess what you are conveying about yourself. Do your clothes give out some particular message ~ that you do a certain job; like a certain style of music; belong to some subculture etc? Does your choice of clothing, jewellery etc convey any particular message about your financial status? How about your hairstyle?

Do you have any tattoos visible to the casual observer? If so, what do these say about you?

What message does your actual body convey, such as in terms of your diet, exercise regime, use of sun-beds or exotic holidays etc?

If you have a friend that you are studying this course with, compare notes. What do you read into each other's appearance? What do you interpret by each other's walk, mannerisms, accent, speech patterns etc?

Though we no longer live in the type of tribes that existed 2000 years ago, our whole appearance and manner conveys endless subtle cues about our self-confidence, education, career, marital status, nationality, religion etc. Some of these cues are things we conscious try to impress upon other people, whilst other cues we probably have no idea we are giving off. What is your appearance telling other people about your place in the modern "tribe"?

Additionally, give some consideration to the *tuarasdal* ritual described earlier. Think about those people to whom you owe a debt of gratitude, the ones whose kindness or generosity you particularly appreciate. It may not be practical to gather them all together in one place, but acquire or make some small gifts for each of these people and dedicate them to the gods before distributing them as an expression of thanks.

Chapter Seven

Values, Morals and Ideals

Judaism and Christianity have the Ten Commandments, but there are no comparable rules carved into stone that Druids must follow. If such things ever existed, they have long since been lost to the mists of time. However, this does not mean that our ancient spiritual ancestors lacked in morality ~ far from it.

The ethical standards of the old tribes formed the basis of their law codes. The oldest surviving version of such a code is the Irish Laws of the Fenechus, also called the Brehon laws (*brehon* being the name for a judge). Thought to go back to ancient times, the first code was supposed to have been composed by a king called Eochaid, also known as the *Ollamh Fodla* (an old name for Ireland) who was believed by the compilers of synthetic histories to have become king in about 633BCE. There is some speculation as to whether he was an historical king, a legendary figure, or maybe even a euhemerised version of the Dagda himself (who shares the title of Eochaid, though this was quite a common name). The 6th century warrior-poet Cennfaelad revamped the laws again about 1000 years later. These laws continued into the increasingly Christian period, and were gradually adapted to the changing morals of the new religion. Some of these changes are easily identifiable; the Church might have introduced others we can only guess at.

An example of a known Christian introduction is the Law of Adamnán, or "Law of the Innocents" as it is sometimes called, brought in by the saint of the same name in 697CE. This law put a stop to women being conscripted into warfare (prior to that date they had been expected to serve as warriors). Tradition has it that the saint introduced this change in law at the behest of his mother Ronait, who was horrified to see female warriors hacking each other up on the battlefield. We have no idea how the average woman at the time viewed this change in law ~ whether they were relieved not to have to fight anymore, or if they felt disempowered by this withdrawal of the duty. Clearly the older Pagan culture had seen nothing immoral in the idea of women being warriors.

As said, there is a bit of guesswork in trying to figure out which laws are of Pagan and which of Christian origin. It is probable that those laws that have no obvious origin within biblical teaching may well have already existed in Ireland before the missionaries arrived. However, there might also have been very old laws that were in keeping with Church policy, and so continued long after most of the Druids had died out.

We will examine the laws of marriage in a later lesson, but suffice to say for now that the Fenechus allowed for nine types of marriage. This is not found elsewhere in Christendom (especially not those types of marriage that allow for financial control to reside with the wife), so it seems likely that those styles of marriage stemmed from the Pagan era, and reflect Pagan views of sex, gender, family values etc.

The Fenechus includes laws that applied across the whole of Ireland (*cain*) and some that only applied to certain areas (*urradas*) ~ this can be viewed as similar to the difference between Federal and State law in America. As with any legal system, there would have been plenty of change ~ even during the pre-Christian era new laws would have been introduced, old ones dropped or amended. The different *urradas* for each province would have reflected different views on the proper way to behave etc. So it is unlikely that there was ever one single stance on what Druids would have constituted ethical behaviour.

The purpose of studying old laws and morals is not so that we can follow them mindlessly like sheep. Merely because a tribesman 2500 years ago thought something was moral does not mean we have to do so today. Rather, our own morals must be reached through reflection and the application of reason. This reflection can be aided by considering the way others have reached their conclusions ~ including how the ancient British and Irish did so.

We know from the stomach contents of unearthed bodies that at least some people in the old tribes ate a lot of meat. Clearly vegetarianism was not an issue for them. However, a modern Druid should feel free to opt for such a diet if they feel it is right to do so. Modern farming methods are quite different, and so the moral choices are different for us in the 21st century. Modern technology has created ethical choices for us that simply didn't exist for the old Druids and their tribes. We each have to decide for ourselves where we stand on issues like stem cell research, vivisection, nuclear energy etc.

One of the central themes that crops up again and again in the Fenechus is that of reparation. A person found guilty of breaking the law was expected to pay some form of compensation to his or her victim. The judge deemed that the victim had lost something of worth ~ property stolen, health broken, good named besmirched etc. A value was placed upon the loss (based to an extent on the social class of the victim) and the convict had to pay up. As well as paying the victim, often the guilty party had to give some money towards the family and any influential patrons. In the case of murder, obviously the victim could not be recompensed, so the money went to the family.

Given that compensation underpinned the law, it may be supposed that it was an important ethical value in daily life too. If a person had done wrong it may well have been thought insufficient for them to apologise or to wring their hands with guilt. Instead they should look to a way to set right what they had done wrong. This is the stance we take in our Clan, and encourage new members to reflect on. It cuts in two directions.

Firstly, a member might consider such harm as they have done and try to rectify it. For example, a person cuts down a tree to build a garden wall. The spirits of the garden may feel the loss; so a few extra trees could be planted as compensation. Where it is no longer possible (or welcome) to recompense directly to the individual affected, people can instead think about a more indirect payback to the universe at large. A driver runs over a collarless dog, with no idea as to who the owner is, and so decides to make a donation of money, time, food etc to a local animal shelter for stray dogs instead.

Secondly, if you are the victim of someone else's malice, then rather than just kicking their teeth in, you could think about ways they could recompense you. They may be willing to do this, if they have a change of heart after the event. Often they may not care, and then it becomes harder to see the balance restored. A corollary from this is that one has to be prepared to allow others the chance to pay back, where they are willing to do so. This is not the same as forgiving someone, nor does it mean you have to be bosom buddies ~ just that, if they acknowledge they have done wrong, that they be allowed to perform some service which clears the debt that they owe you. This may be particularly hard if the "crime" was a horrible one, and you genuinely wish to have no further contact with them. Perhaps they could be allowed to redress the balance by giving money to a charity, or helping some third party that you have nominated?

The Fenechus provided guidance on ways of seeking redress from an individual who refused to pay their fines. One of these ways was called *troscad*, or hunger strike. The victim would sit outside the house of the offender and starve themselves, telling all who passed what they were doing and why. This brought shame on the offender, and often resulted in many people refusing to trade with them because they had lost the trust of the community. A few decades back many Irish prisoners held during the Troubles went on hunger strikes to protest against the British government. Earlier still, many Suffragettes tried the same.

The *troscad* only really works if the person being protested against (and the community witnessing the act) understands the nature of what is happening. In the case of the prisoners, the British government really didn't care, many members of the newspaper-reading public didn't understand what was going on, and so the starvation was less effective than it might have been otherwise.

We wouldn't recommend people risk their health trying *troscad* today. However, the underlying theme is important ~ that justice is in the hands of us all. Justice is not something that anonymous people in government make happen. We all make the world a just place (or unjust, if we are so inclined). If someone treated a Gael unfairly, it was her moral duty to do something about it, rather than to just crawl into a corner like a whipped dog. It was also the duty of the wider community to pay attention to such protests and respond accordingly.

This is further reflected with the idea of *digal*. In a previous lesson we discussed how Gaelic society was once run by *flaithe* (aristocrats) who had their clients, or *céile*. If a *céile* were attacked, robbed, raped or whatever, then they could seek support of their *flaith* in bringing the miscreant to justice. Conversely, if the *flaith* were the victim, then they could call upon all their *céile* to battle against the offender until justice was done. This feud was called a *digal*, and again was considered a moral duty. If a patron, friend or relative had been victimised by someone who appeared to be getting away with it, then the tribe were expected to rally round and bring the criminal to book. Failure to act would have been considered reprehensible.

In the modern day a great many people get involved in political campaigns to pressure governments, big businesses etc into behaving ethically. This is a similar sort of notion to *digal* ~ the idea that everyone associated with a cause has to take action to bear down on some wrongdoer until they agree to change their ways.

Implicit in the idea of *digal* is that there must be an end to it.

Those campaigning for justice must have a clear idea of how they want the wrongdoer to act, and be prepared to let bygones be bygones once they have capitulated. To start a feud without any clear way for it to be resolved peacefully would have been considered misguided. The idea wasn't to seek revenge, but to seek justice.

One myth that reflects this is that of the Sons of Tuirenn. Tuirenn's three sons killed Lugh's father, and he demanded compensation of them (called *eric*, or blood-money). They completed all the impossible tasks that he set them but, at the end, he still contrived to kill them anyway. This, the myth makes clear, was considered a bit of a poor show ~ that Lugh should have accepted their compensation without seeking yet further vengeance.

Another source of information about what the old Celts might have considered ethical can be found in the myths. One particular set of stories concerns the *Fianna*, a band of Robin Hood-type warriors lead by Fionn Mac Cumhall. Though described as a warrior chief, the myths may well have been based on tales of a god. The name Fionn means holy or sacred, and there are Iron Age altars to gods with names like Vindos and Vindonnus (which *may* be old names for the same god.) There is also a cognate Welsh figure, Gwyn, who has divine qualities and bears a lot of similarity to the Irish hunter.

The motto of the *Fianna*, which all the warriors swore by, runs;

Strength in our hands,
Truth in our hearts,
Fulfilment on our lips.

Some translators will give slightly different words, but the underlying meaning is much the same. It is down to the individual to decide what this means, but I will give you the understanding we have come to in our Clan as a starting point.

Strength in our hands is not about big muscles, but about courage and having the bravery to face up to an enemy. That applies not just to warriors bashing each other with swords, but to facing any kind of fear and overcoming it. It also strikes us as being about emotional courage in the face of rejection, loss, grief etc. There are people in the world who retreat into a shell and seldom come out ~ painfully shy, fearful of being hurt, timid and repressed. Such outlooks are quite alien to the myths, which are full of people who grab life with both hands and live it to the full. For us, this strength is that which comes from living fully, passionately, and energetically.

Truth in our hearts is echoed by other maxims about the importance of truth. One relatively modern Welsh saying, attributed to Iolo Morgannwg, is *"truth against the world"* ~ standing up for what you know to be true even if everyone else thinks you are wrong. A much older Irish saying is, *'three candles illumine every darkness: truth, nature, knowledge.'* Truth within the heart suggests that it is most important to know truth, more so than to speak it. Truth can be used to hurt people, if it is blunt and harsh. If someone asks 'do I look fat in this dress', then telling him or her that they look like a beached whale may be true, but it is unnecessarily cruel. Truth can be put across diplomatically. The Druids often went as diplomats, and so must have been used to putting the truth across in a gentle manner that wouldn't stir up more trouble.

Fulfilment on our lips seems, to us, to be about eloquence. Language can be a beautiful thing, and can be used to make your own and other peoples lives more pleasurable. Further, the twin duties of the *fili* (poet) are to praise and satirise. If someone does an honourable deed, the bard sings of it. This is not a matter of brown-nosing. If the deed is done in silence, others will not hear of it, will not be inspired to follow suit, the good (as it were) will not spread. Also, a person who receives praise is far more likely to act well in future than one who is constantly overlooked or ignored. Likewise, a dishonourable act that goes unremarked leaves others ignorant to the nature of the perpetrator and so vulnerable to abuse. Also, others contemplating similar acts may feel emboldened that they can act as abysmally as they wish and get no comeuppance. Satire is a form of justice for the victim, a public acknowledgement that what was done to them was indeed wrong. The power of public ridicule remains strong today ~ one need only think of certain successful comedians and impressionists who have made a successful career highlighting the failings of politicians. The fulfilment of the lips is not really about using elaborate words, but about speaking out ~ praising what is good, satirising what is bad, having the confidence to ask questions or express ideas. Silence, for the old tribes, was not particularly golden!

One of the major Celtic virtues, spoken of again and again, was hospitality. In early Ireland each household was expected to provide food, warmth and entertainment to any guest that arrived peacefully at their door. As time went by these duties devolved onto particular people, the *brugaid*, who were awarded farmland with which to sustain and run free hostels for travellers called *brugh*. Some hostels appear to have been geared for high-class visitors and others for ordinary travellers. These hostelries were probably developed to avoid crippling financial burdens on ordinary householders whose guests overstayed their welcome. The law specifically stated:

All members of the tribe are required to offer hospitality to strangers. The only exceptions are minor children, madmen, and old people.

The above reference to old people was primarily to those who had become very frail ~ it was a common practice to distribute the wealth of such a person to their family, rather like an early inheritance. Most tribal cultures value hospitality towards guests, with the offering of food and drink as a matter of course. Many cultures have myths about the Gods disguising themselves as wayfarers in order to test the generosity of people. Hospitality is not just about feeding people, but about making them feel welcome and valued. A poor host is one who does not give his guests a second thought, but largely ignores them. In Irish myth Bres, a chieftain of the *Tuatha Dé*, was satirised by the poet Cairbre for being stingy and neglectful. A bad host is one who goes out of their way to do or say things to make a guest uncomfortable. As well as there being guidance for hosts, so there was for guests on how to behave properly. Not outstaying their welcome being one, and not picking fights with their host another.

Hospitality overlapped into generosity generally. A chieftain maintained the loyalty of his warriors by making gifts to them from the spoils of war. One of the biggest insults to a person was to call them mean ~ such as the character from medieval Welsh myth who was known as Brân the Niggard. The value of generosity remained important well into medieval and later times. The importance behind the giving of gifts and the entertaining of visitors was to make people feel valued and wanted; to celebrate life; to keep strong ties within the tribe and with potential allies. These are just some of the values that shine out of the old laws.

Some questions for you to think about:

- Are there any actions that you consider to be always bad or immoral? Are there any actions that are always good or desirable?
- Can you think of ways in which the issue of making compensation might effect your own life... either where you were the victim, or the offender?
- To what extent do modern people have a responsibility for making justice happen? Is justice now entirely the preserve of the State?

Practical exercise:

Think of a situation in which you have deliberately or accidentally wounded another person by depriving them of something ~ health, material possessions, self-confidence, a relationship etc. Try to find a way to compensate them for this loss. This could be something you may wish to discuss with others within your group, if you have one, or wider circle of friends. Compensation can be in the form of money or, like Setanta taking the role of Culain's dead hound, in the form of service. There may be other ways in which an injured party can be recompensed.

If you cannot think of any such situation, then consider the impact you have on the environment and make a gift back to the Land for whatever it is that you have most recently taken from it.

Additionally reflect on the value of hospitality by either hosting a meal (if you are a good cook) for Pagan friends who will understand the significance of the gesture or (if you're incompetent in the kitchen) by taking them out to dinner.

Chapter Eight

The Festivals

Whilst there is a reasonable amount of evidence for medieval festivals, we have scant evidence for how the pre-Christian Celts celebrated their high days and holy days. A small hint comes to us from the period when Christian and Pagan lived side-by-side in ancient Gaul. St Martin of Tours, according to his biographer Severus, encountered a funeral procession bearing a corpse in a winding sheet. The saint disrupted the sad event, thinking it was a Druid festival. Severus records:

> it was the custom of the Gallic rustics in their wretched folly to carry about through the fields the images of demons veiled with a white covering.

This brings to mind accounts of Germanic processions involving a statue of the goddess Nerthus concealed within a cart. The context is now gone ~ was the statue at some stage unveiled, was it being carried from one temple to another, was it being brought to a specific village to work a miracle (break a drought, heal a plague etc), and so forth. That St Martin had a concept of these parades suggests he had seen one before, i.e. that they were at least semi-regular events. It may be that processions of veiled statues were peculiar to Gaul, or that they also happened in other Celtic areas.

A contemporary Druid group might wish to emulate such an event, carrying a shrouded statue or image from one sacred place to another (or simply on a circular route to and from the same location, perhaps marking the boundary of an important area of land).

Historians often discuss both the antiquity of the Gaelic

festivals and whether the early Brythonic Celts (Welsh, Cornish and Bretons) would have held exactly the same festivals as their Goidelic cousins. At the moment, the jury still seems to be out as to the likelihood of that. For the purpose of brevity, we will focus this lesson on the evidence we have for how the Goidelic tribes of Ireland, Scotland and the Isle of Man celebrated the turning festivals of the year. Some additional material will be included from Brythonic sources, but a more detailed look at those sources will take place in a future lesson.

There is good evidence to suggest that the medieval Gaels marked four major festivals each year, which were common to most (perhaps all) tribes. It is commonly believed that these four festivals pre-date Christianity, but textual sources to confirm this are scant. Individual tribes may also have had their own local festivals that were not adhered to in other parts of the land.

Let us start with the early winter festival of Samhain. Manuscripts describe this as a seven-day festival in late October/early November. There is much talk about feasting, game playing and the like. There are no clear descriptions of what rituals took place at this time. However, we can look at myths to see what sorts of stories are set at this time of year. We must again bear in mind that most of these myths were being committed to writing in the 9th to 12th centuries, and it may be argued that the medieval notion as to what a festival was about is not necessarily an accurate reflection of how people 500 years beforehand saw those same celebrations.

The 11th century 'Birth of Áed Sláine' describes the feast of Samhain as *"the pagans' Easter"*. This could perhaps allude to the Pagan event reminding the scribe of the death of Jesus. It may be wondered if Samhain were originally a general feast for all ancestors, or if perhaps it started out as the commemoration of the death of one specific person. Equally the scribe may have been considering Easter as a festival of resurrection, and implying that Samhain was also a time for the dead to return ~ maybe in terms of having a single night to visit their descendants, or perhaps it even being the main night on which souls might be thought of as having a chance to reincarnate.

The *Tuatha Dé Danann* arrived on Beltaine (like the people of Cesair and Partholon before them), and fought their first great battle against the *Fir Bolg* soon after. The major, defining battle though was the Second Conflict on the Plain of Pillars. Waged against the loathsome *Fomóiri*, this war is described as occurring on Samhain. One of the reasons being that Samhain was the time chosen by the *Fomóiri* for demanding their onerous taxes of the subjugated *Tuatha Dé*. In an image reminiscent of the Poll Tax riots, the people of Danu rose up and overthrew the tyrants. When Lugh slew the terrible Balor, the tide of battle was finally turned in favour of the incoming deities.

From this we might surmise that Samhain was a popular time for the making of offerings, both to deities and perhaps to more temporal powers. Yet the destruction of the gruesome children of Domnu suggests a theme of liberation, of throwing off unfair or oppressive forces. Whilst November may well be the start of winter, with all its imagery of greyness and gloom, this tale gives us a metaphor of dynamism and freedom.

A somewhat similar tale can be found in the story of the destruction of Tara. A bard of the *Sídhe* called Aillen mac Midgna stalks out of the hill of Finnachaid and casts a sleep-spell over the inhabitants of Tara using a musical instrument. Each Samhain night for 23 years (or in some versions nine years) his fiery breath burned the hall to the ground, and it had to be rebuilt over the winter. This continued until the time when the young hero Fionn Mac Cumhail, arriving for the Feast of Tara, stuck a spear through him. As with the previous tale, a dangerous and oppressive force is overthrown ~ a curious image that many might find at odds with the usual perception of a coming winter, especially in former times bereft of central heating and thermal underwear! It might be conjectured that, despite the physical harshness of winter, that season was not perceived in a negative manner at all, but seen as a time of release.

At a practical level Samhain was the time when the Fianna, the warrior bands such as the one lead by Fionn, stopped fighting and quartered with the families they had spent all summer protecting. The battles in Samhain myths might just reflect the desire of hardened fighters to have one last good punch-up before sheathing their swords for the winter holidays. It may also reflect the notion of winter as a time of peace, when theoretically the Fianna would not be needed. By contrast many of the Beltane myths, when the warriors' hostelling ceased, are tales of conquest and glory seeking.

In other stories of Fionn the mounds of the *Sídhe*, which archaeologists have long since shown to be burial chambers from the Bronze Age and earlier, were revealed to human eyes. Normally the magical nature of these hillocks was concealed by the presence of a veil, the *fe-fiada*. On the winter feast all became shown for its true nature. The leader of the warrior bands of Leinster got to see not just inside the mounds, but also witnessed their inhabitants riding forth. One might ask if the native tribes of 2000-odd years ago were aware that the mounds contained corpses. If they were, then the beings riding forth were probably seen as ghosts of some sort. If they were unaware of the original purpose of the mounds, then they might well have conceived of this as a festival of land-spirits, rather than of the returning dead (though, of course, those two concepts are not mutually exclusive). Successive waves of colonisers to Irish and British shores have re-used older burial chambers to inter their own dead, so it seems quite likely that Celtic tribes would have been fully aware that there were decaying bones inside the *sídhe*-mounds.

The story of Nera has a decidedly spectral touch to it. On Samhain, King Ailill offered rewards to anyone brave enough to put a wicker band around the foot of a hanging corpse. Only Nera was courageous / daft enough to volunteer. Approaching the corpse, it animated and asked for water. Bizarrely, Nera allowed it to climb on to his back and carried it to a house, around which flames sprang up. They tried another house, which was then surrounded by water. The third attempt proved safer, and the corpse drank three cups worth, spitting the last out on the house-holders, killing them. Going back to court, Nera found the palace on fire and the inhabitants decapitated. Nera rushed to the Cave of Cruachan, located in County Roscommon, in search of the severed heads. He met a ban-sidhe, who revealed that it was just a vision of what might be (sort of like the Ghost of Samhain Yet to Come). To prevent this happening he was advised to demolish the hill. To do this he called on Fergus mac Roigh, but escaped with the *Sídhe* woman. Samhain night, then, could be a time of visions and warnings, a time to meet the dead ~ but be aware that the dead are not always pleasant!

The Cave of Cruachan also has its own story of another monster called Aillen. This one had three heads, and caused no end of mayhem until despatched at Samhain by Amairgin. The burial ground of Daithi, considered by many to be the last Pagan king of Ireland, lies not far away, and it is possible that the monstrous nature of Cruachan may have built up in the minds of Christian storytellers because of that. The fortress at Cruachan was the seat of power of such luminaries as Queen Medb, and something of a focal point for the province of Connacht (modern Connaught).

Another Connacht hero, Cascorach, encountered bizarre Samhain spirits at Cruachan. An old servant called Bairnech bewailed the fact that a woman of the *Sídhe* left the cave each November eve and whisked away nine of the best animals in every herd. The *Fomóiri* demanded tribute of a third of the *Tuatha Dé's* grain, milk and first born children, whilst Fionn pledged a third of his trophies to his aide Fiachra at Samhain ~ suggestive that three (and in this case thrice three) may have been a relevant unit for the making of offerings, willing or otherwise. One of the kennings for the ogam letter *Tinne* is a third part, perhaps a link between that few and sacrifice. Cascorach despatched the *ban-sidhe* without resistance, once again with a spear. No sooner was this problem dealt with, than the old man complained of three female werewolves who also appeared out of the cave and mangled the local sheep population. Cascorach tricked the lycan-thropes into resuming their human guise in order to listen to his harp music (the equally feral Mis was also lured by the harp music of the bard Dubh Ruis), whereupon his friend Caoilte skewered them with a spear. A good deal of spearing goes on in these tales, which may itself have some symbolic importance.

King Aillil might have been nicer to the land spirits when choosing a pasture for his horses. The *Sidhe*, whose land it was, felt affronted by his action (perhaps he didn't ask them nicely first) and so, at Samhain, blasted the grass that the horses fed on. To add insult to injury, the king then raped one of the *Sidhe* women, Aine, who had cursed the field. She responded by cutting his ear off, whereupon he killed her. The *Sidhe*, eager for vengeance, created a magical yew tree. The desire to possess this tree was such that a great battle was fought between vying factions from local tribes. Amongst those slaughtered were Aillil and most of his family. Let this be a lesson ~ play nicely with the land spirits, or else!

On a stranger level the burly deity the Dagda is described as having sex with the Morrighan, by mounting her when she had one ankle on either bank of the River Unius! This has led some commentators to suggest that fertility rites took place at Samhain (whether in or out of a river, no-one seems willing to say). This may be the case, though the ribald nature of so many myths conveys the sense that those old tribes didn't need much of an excuse for a bit of fertility at any time of the year.

On a more romantic note, Samhain was the time when Óengus mac Óg finally met his dream-lover Caer in the flesh. Though it might be more apposite to say in the feather, given that she has been transformed into a swan by the time he found her. Close to dying from a wasting illness, Óengus opted to transform himself into a swan that he might be with his ladylove. Each Samhain she turns from swan to maiden or back again, and he changes himself in accordance. A cynic might note that the fact that a man willingly changes himself to please a woman proves that this is a myth! Nonetheless, it gives a powerful image of self-sacrifice ~ Óengus prepared to give up everything for love. This echoes, in a more pleasant fashion, the *Tuatha Dé* having to pay their price to the demanding *Fomóiri* overlords. To everything there is a cost, and at Samhain it must be paid ~ or refuted through bloodshed.

Another tale which links Óengus to events at Samhain is that of the maiden Enghi, who had fallen in love with the handsome god, though she had never seen him (rather as he fell for Caer, whom he knew only from a dream). Enghi tried to find the object of her desire at a Samhain gathering, only to be kidnapped by the *Sídhe*. The tales so often imply that the *Sídhe* really do not like to leave empty-handed on Samhain.

Many (though by no means all[25]) sources argue that Samhain derives its name from the same root as the Gaulish month of Samonios, as described on the Coligny Calendar. Those theorists who dissent from this stance claim that Samonios signifies not the end of summer, but its beginning, and is not in November, but May ~ therefore the three-day feast marked on the Coligny tablets refers to Beltane. This, it is argued, is the true New Year's Day. It is certainly not explicitly stated anywhere in early myths that Samhain is definitely the start of the year, and the story of the *Tuatha Dé* arriving in Ireland on Beltane would be an appropriate image for an inaugural feast. However, the subsequent month on the Coligny calendar is called Dumannios, probably deriving from a root word meaning black or dark ~ suitable for December, less so for June. So, whilst not absolutely definite, it seems quite likely that the three-day Gaulish feast of Samonios was going on at the same time as the Gaelic feast of Samhain. If it opened the year in Gaul, it may well have done so in other Celtic regions too.

We know that a number of the Neolithic stone circles and monuments were aligned with the winter and summer solstices. Clearly these dates had a big enough importance to warrant major building projects. However, we don't know for sure if these dates retained importance into the Iron Age. There don't appear to be many surviving myths set at either solstice, and most of the folk practices seem to be of Christian or Norse origin.

In Scotland midwinter is called *An Fheill-Shlinnein*, which derives from the word for a type of divination involving looking at the cracks formed in a burnt ox bone. Presumably this act of divination comes from Pagan sources, though whether Celtic or Norse is unclear. Another intriguing aspect of Scottish lore is the habit of carving a log into the shape of an old woman, the *cailleach-nollag*, and then burning it. This may well be connected to a festival held to the wintry goddess Cailleach on or near the solstice.

On the Isle of Man, up until fairly recent times, the summer solstice was marked by carrying bundles of straw to the top of certain hills as a gift to Manannán mac Lir, god of the sea. He would sometimes favour his devotees by appearing in the guise of a crane. The goddess sometimes described as his wife, Aine, was also honoured at the solstice in some parts of Ireland by the carrying of burning bundles of straw up mountainsides. One late dated myth described Aine, by then thought of as a fairy queen, feeding the starving during the Great Hunger.

The First Battle of Moy Tuiredh, fought between the *Tuatha Dé* and the *Fir Bolg*, was meant to take place at midsummer. It would therefore be at this time that Nuada, then king of the *Tuatha Dé*, lost his hand and kingship whilst fighting Sreng.

Whatever the exact origins of these slivers of folklore, we cannot be certain of the two solstices significance to Iron Age Celts (but that doesn't stop modern Druids holding whatever sort of ritual they like at these times). There do not appear to be any accounts of myths or gatherings taking place at either of the two equinoxes. Perhaps these simply weren't important by the Iron Age?

A few days prior to the winter solstice, on 18th December, the Romans held a festival called the Eponalia. This was dedicated to the Celtic horse goddess Epona, much admired by the Roman cavalry. It is possible that their choice of this date was based on some older festival held on that day by one or more Celtic tribes.

The festival of Imbolc or Oimelc (probably deriving from the word for sheep's milk) takes place at the start of February. On the ancient Roman calendar February was a month for spring-cleaning and purification rituals. Many statues were taken out of the temples and cleaned. The Christian church kept up this practice, and made the festival of Saint Brigit on February 2nd one of light and cleanliness. Whilst there almost certainly was a real woman called Abbess Brigit who lived in Kildare, many of the stories associated with her have their roots in myths about the Pagan goddess of the same name. Christian tradition has it that the monastery founded by the Abbess was co-habiting (back then Irish nuns and monks could marry and have children), but that an area of the grounds contained a perpetually burning fire which only women could tend or go near. In his *Topographia Hibernie,* Giraldus Cambrensis referred to a sisterhood of 19 nuns tending the flame. Subsequent to the abbess' death, the Giraldus said the nuns continued to hold a 19-day vigil with the flame going untended on the twentieth day as this was when the ghost of the sainted Brigit took charge at the bequest of. *'Brigid, tend your fire. This is your night.'* It is debatable if this has any basis within the Christian religion, so we can but assume that these practices went back to Pagan times and were simply absorbed into the Church. The flame remained until 1540, when it was forcibly extinguished. The idea of a sisterhood tending a holy flame certainly goes back to the temples of Vesta and Hestia in ancient Rome and

Greece respectively. In Bricriu's number ogam, the number 19 is linked to the letter *Eadha*, usually given as the aspen or poplar tree. That tree does not appear in the Brigit stories, but it is possible that there may have been some symbolism attached to the letter/number. Nineteen years is also the period of the Meton Cycle, which has astronomical significance for Druids, and may have been the basis for Caesar's claim that Druids took two decades to train.

Early February is not a pleasant time for travel (being cold and wet), and there are no surviving records of big feasts or fairs at Imbolc. Most likely it was a fairly quiet, homely festival.

One of the few myths set at this time is an episode in the *Táin Bó Cúailnge* in which the great warrior Cú Chulainn was single-handedly holding off the armies of Queen Medb. He went for months without rest, fighting day and night. Close to dying of exhaustion, his father Lugh appeared at Imbolc and put him into a magical, healing sleep. Lugh himself then kept the armies at bay. Perhaps Imbolc may have been seen as a time for renewal of body and soul.

In agricultural terms, early February is lambing season ~ a vital period for ancient communities who had been surviving on preserved meat and grain. Many people must have breathed a sigh of relief to have fresh milk and meat again.

There are very late recorded Scottish myths set at this time in which an elderly goddess, the Cailleach, either drinks from a magical well and becomes young, or in which she battles against (and loses her fight with) the youthful goddess Brigit. Some historians have questioned how old these particular legends are, but they remain widespread and, in our experience, have earned the approval of both deities when told in ritual. There are a variety of caves around Scotland and the province of Munster that are said to be inhabited by the Cailleach when she hibernates over the warmer months. The presence of a holly staff outside the cave indicates she is at rest.

Beltaine (or Cétshamain, as it is sometimes called) opens the summer, and with it the battle season. Those warriors who had been wintering with families returned to their nomadic life in forests and fields. Wars started up again. Appropriately enough the *Partholonians*, *Tuatha Dé Danann* and the *Milesians* all arrived in Ireland to conquer the land at Beltane.

Linguists argue backwards and forwards as to the origin of the word Beltaine ~ whether it refers generally to "bright fires" or is a more direct reference to the deity Belenus, whom some interpret as a sun god and others as a healing deity (and some as both!) Belenus means 'Bright One', so the name of the festival might take its bright element either from his name or from a general use of that adjective. This was certainly a popular time for bonfires, often with cattle being driven between two fires in order to purge parasites and confer good yields.

Traditionally a Beltaine fire was kindled on the Hill of Uisnech, the first one having been lit by a Druid of the *Nemedians*. Seven other Druids objected to what he was doing, so he cut their tongues out and buried them in the hill. Hopefully this is meant to be taken as a metaphor ~ perhaps that the Druid Mide had won over the opinions of the others (so their tongues wagged for him rather than against him)? In a culture where magic was seen as heavily oral in nature, it may also be that he gained their magical powers for himself. That there were seven tongues may be just a random number, or have significance to either history (seven tribes united in a common cause) or mysticism (the number seven links to the ogam letter *Duir* - the oak tree, much associated with kingship and gaining prestige or power.) Or, as mentioned earlier in the book, it could be a Christian analogy to the seven tiers of the Church or the seven ranks of the *filid* that they inspired.

King Aillil and his mistress engaged is some suitably licentious behaviour at Beltaine. Sadly for them, the warrior Conall leapt out from behind a bush and killed them both.

Perhaps more profoundly, the young Fionn Mac Cumhail was

set to tend the cooking of the magical salmon at Beltaine for the old Druid Finéces. Juices from the fish spurted out and landed on his fingers, which he unthinkingly sucked to cool them off. He was then allowed to eat and imbibe all the magical powers of the fish. The story is remarkably similar to the Welsh tale of Taliesin, though that story is not set at any particular time of the year (at least, not in the versions that survived in manuscript form). Having also gained the power of prophecy by accidentally drinking water from a magical well, Fionn composed a long poem singing the praises of the month of May and all the changes that come upon nature during that time. The poem begins ~

> *May-day, season surpassing!*
> *Splendid is colour then.*
> *Blackbirds sing a full lay,*
> *if there be a slender shaft of day.*
> *The dust-coloured cuckoo calls aloud:*
> *Welcome, splendid summer!*
> *The bitterness of bad weather is past,*
> *the boughs of the wood are a thicket.*

Beltaine, then, was probably seen as a joyful time but also a time of risk and high adventure. Unexpected gifts and serendipitous events might occur at this time.

In Wales this festival is called Calan Mai, and is associated with several myths. The horse goddess Rhiannon had her newborn child stolen by a mysterious beast who also tried to kidnap a mare's foal on this date. She was falsely accused of having eaten her own child, but eventually exonerated. The huntsman god Gwyn ap Nudd does annual battle with Gwythur, in order to win the favours of Creiddylad. On the Isle of Man there is also a mythical battle, but between two women ~ the Queen of Summer and the Queen of Winter (naturally, the first one is the winner). The latter myths can be seen largely as fairly overt metaphors for seasonal shifts. The loss of the child and the subsequent unjust punishment placed upon Rhiannon bear deeper contemplation.

Lughnasadh takes place in early August, and according to myth was started by the god Lugh as a means of honouring his *Fir Bolg* foster-mother Tailtiu. She had died of exhaustion after clearing many forests in Connaught for agriculture. Given the proximity of the harvest, it may be suggested that Tailtiu's collapse is an image of the earth giving her all through the harvest, and then dying over winter. Another funeral feast associated with this time was that of a little-known goddess called Carmen, for whom a commemorative fair was held every three years. A more prominent goddess, Macha, who died as the result of being goaded into a foot race by her idiotic husband, was also honoured with a fair or *oénach* at this time. The death of a great woman crops up again and again at Lughnasadh. In the known stories of Tailtiu and Macha, both died doing the honourable thing to benefit others. Modern Druids might wish to pause a while at this feast and think of the countless mothers, wives, sisters etc who have worked themselves into an early grave caring for families, or by professionally caring as nurses, doctors, soldiers etc.

Whilst most of the other magical races arrived in Ireland at Beltaine, Tailtiu's people landed at the August feast. It may be that the ancestral tribes of Connaught (supposedly descended from the *Fir Bolg*) attached a significance to Lughnasadh that was quite distinct from its meaning to the other tribes of Ireland.

Lughnasadh, sometimes also called *Bron Trogain*, was a popular time for making temporary marriages. These would often last only until Imbolc, and would serve as a means of people supporting and comforting each other over the harsh winter. Even if the marriage was dissolved, legal responsibility remained for any children of the union.

Of equal popularity were the horse races that took place at the great Lughnasadh fairs. The invention of racing was attributed to

Lugh himself, as was the board game *fidchell* (a bit like chess). This was a widely indulged activity over this festival period.

The meaning of any festival changes over time and place, gaining new significances and loosing old associations. It would be odd for a 21st century city dweller to try and re-enact exactly the style of festival held by a 3rd century cattle baron. In understanding these festivals it is important to focus on the underlying themes and try to apply them to your own life in the modern age ~ what these times of year, qualities and events signify to you now.

There is also no reason why modern practitioners should be restricted to only marking events that we suppose were important to the farmers of 2000 years ago. If you are a gardener or smallholder, there may be times of the year of overt significance to you based on the type of crop, flower or livestock that you rear. If you live in a coastal area and depend on fishing for a livelihood, the tides of the fish you harvest are likely to be of import.

So far we have mostly discussed festivities based around events in the natural world. It is also quite acceptable to mark other types of occasion ~ the founding of your ritual group, the date you emigrated to a new homeland, the anniversary of a significant death or birth etc.

Festivals of whatever sort are a time to remember who we are, where we have come from, to whom (or what) we owe loyalty and gratitude, what we truly depend upon. Though festivals can be celebrated alone, they are mostly social occasions for reinforcing bonds of love, fealty, and mutual respect.

Some questions for you to think about:

- Have you attended a Celtic festival (either a Pagan one or some form of cultural gathering) in the past? If so, what did you think of it? If you have never attended such a gathering, would you like to do so in the future?
- Which festival do you most like the sound of, and in what ways might you try and celebrate it?

- Think about whether you prefer to celebrate festivals by yourself or with other people. Do the changing seasons affect your moods? Perhaps you feel more sociable at some times of the year than others, or more inclined to certain activities than others etc.

Practical exercise:

Create a new seasonal festival to celebrate by yourself or with friends. Consider what is important to you or the place where you live. If you live by the coast, you could create a festival to mark an important event in the fishing world. If you have a favourite animal, you could mark some event in their life cycle (such as the breeding season, the time when their young are born etc). If you are an avid gardener or brewer, you could mark an event connected to your favourite flower, the grape vines or so forth.

In creating your festival, think about what this seasonal event means to you, where best to hold the event (somewhere directly connected to the event being marked), any associated deities, what sort of things you could do during the ritual to express how important this event is etc.

Try to keep notes as to what you did and why (and the outcome), so that you can refer back to it in future.

Chapter Nine

Young People

The early book of Gaelic legal codes called the Law of the Fenechus (referred to in Chapter Seven) had guidance to give on the matter of family life, as well as on most other things! As discussed before, family was terrifically important to the Celtic peoples, from early times onwards. The law was quite clear in terms of what was expected of people, with regards to how they cared for each other. In this lesson we will look at the treatment of the young, and of those still in education. In future lessons we will explore other aspects of tribal life. The purpose of this lesson is partly to flesh out the historical background to the religious ideas, but also to stimulate reflection on how we organise modern Society, and the ways we could change it in future.

Cormac's Glossary (which was written by a bishop who lived in Cashel in the 8th century) details six "ages of man" ~ *naoid-heanachd*, or infancy; *macdacht*, or boyhood (or *inidacht* as the probable word for girlhood); *gillacht*, or youth; *óglachass*, or primacy; *séndatu*, or elderhood; and *dibildeta*, or decrepitude. Women could get married at fourteen, the age at which males were entering into the phase of *gillacht*. Women probably had five "ages", and went straight from childhood into primacy.

Childhood, then, had three phases. By the time the Fenechus was being put in written form, males ceased to be children at the age of seventeen. At this age they could marry (with their family's consent) and hold adult legal status. Whilst the head of the family, the *cenn-fine*, remained alive, they still needed his consent to form business contracts and the like. Whether the ages of consent were the same prior to the 8th century, we do not currently know.

The legal (bearing in mind parents had to pay fines for their children's behaviour) and financial responsibility for raising children was usually divided equally between both parents. There were some exceptions to this. If a man violently raped a woman (*forcor*) or molested her whilst she was too drunk or drugged to know what was happening (*sleth*), then he had to finance the care of any child thus resulting. The *cenn-fine* had to give formal consent to any sexual liaisons embarked on by his or her dependents. If an unmarried female relative had an affair without the *cenn's* consent, and fell pregnant, again the man bore sole financial responsibility. A free man who impregnated a *cumal* (an indentured female servant) bore the care of the child. Conversely, a free woman who became pregnant by a *mug* (a male servant) would have to pay for the care of her child, and take legal burden for it. Such children were considered to be born free, and did not inherit the lowly status of their servant parent.

The mother might also be expected to take sole care if she became pregnant by a foreigner who had no social standing within the tribe. In later periods, as communities became larger and prostitution more common, ladies of the night could make no claims against their customers should they fall with children.

Early Gaelic society seems to have allowed for a degree of social mobility between the classes. However, as the centuries rolled past they seem to have become more oriented to hereditary class. As one law text stated:

Whether the offspring of kings, warriors, poets, workers in wood or stone, or tillers of the soil, a son or daughter shall follow the career of his or her parents.

Thus the expected future of the child became mapped out. The old texts also had something to say on the proper rearing of children. Unsympathetic to the current politically correct outlook, the Brehon laws allowed parents to slap their children up until the age of seven. After that a naughty child was not meant to be hit, but rather was supposed to be subject to punishments in the form of fines on their pocket money. These fines were meant to reflect the measures they could expect when they became adults.

Childhood in 3rd century Ireland would have been very different from one in 21st century Suffolk. Extended families were the norm back then, and aunts, cousins, grandfathers etc would have surrounded most children. Given that most communities were fairly small, children would quite probably have known the names of virtually everyone in their village. There is an African saying that it takes a village to raise a child, and that communal approach would probably have been familiar in ancient times.

It is not currently known if the old tribes had puberty rites to mark the transition to adulthood ~ though these seem to be very common throughout tribal societies. We can look to other cultures to see what they did, such as the Roman habit of adopting adult dress and ceremonially burning items associated with childhood, though whether anything similar was done in these lands we can only guess at. One element that may be guessed at is renaming. A number of heroes were known by one name in childhood, and another when becoming prominent warriors, such as Setanta becoming Cú Chulainn. The names are awarded on the basis of some event, and this may have been a widespread practice.

Some modern social commentators have pointed out that the idea of a rebellious teen is often unusual in tribal societies that have puberty rites. Such writers have suggested that having and important event that draws a line under childhood and confers adult rights and responsibilities may be an important factor in psychological stability. In Britain, there is no simple cut-off age in law (one can get married at 16, but not buy a shot of vodka in a pub) and no widely recognised puberty ritual. Unless one counts getting pissed and shagging a stranger in an alleyway as a modern puberty rite.

Aiteachas, or fosterage, was a major feature of early Celtic culture. The word can also mean to cultivate land ~ to nurture growing things. On entering the stage of *macdacht*, many children were sent to live with foster parents. Some people fostered out of love, a type of guardianship called *altramm serce* ('fostering of love'). Others fostered more as an apprenticeship, getting paid by the parents for the keep of the child ~ and teaching them social or professional skills in the process. The word for a foster-father, *aite*, is also the word for a teacher (*muime* means both foster-mother, and nurse). *Dalta*, a foster child, also means a student or apprentice.

The Gaelic notion of a school was unlike ours. A school was not a building, but a group of people gathered about a teacher. Where the master went, the school followed. As a fosterer fed and housed their ward, so the teacher fed and housed their student. The role of the teacher was to inspire and cultivate. The agricultural allusion encourages the idea of bringing out what is already there, rather than of filling an empty head with endless dates, names, and facts and figures.

With approaching adulthood many youths may have looked towards apprenticeships to learn a craft or profession. Most probably just took up the family trade as the previous quote suggested, but there would have been those who looked to masters outside their blood-kin to teach them a new skill. The surviving Brehon law books describe apprentices ~ be they learning blacksmithing, carpentry, Druidry or whatever ~ as becoming part of the household of their teachers. Just like a foster-parent they became answerable for the students actions in law, were required to authorise such business deals or marriage contracts as the pupil might wish to make etc. The student became a member of the family, not just a virtual stranger who turned up to a class once a week.

In the modern day few people could afford to feed, clothe etc one student, let alone an entire class of them. However, teachers (at least perhaps those operating from a Druid world view) can still be seen as having moral responsibility for their pupils. This need not be just in terms of schoolteachers and kiddies, but also anyone who agrees to teach an adult some skill or knowledge, perhaps especially religious knowledge.

It's no longer viable for the head of a Druidic group or Order to have right of censure over members' marriage plans or mortgages (perish the thought!). However, there is a responsibility for the nature of what is taught. It should be accurate, to the best of everyone's awareness, but also it should be delivered in a responsible and caring way. Poor teachers rely on fear and humiliation to get their points across. Students, even (perhaps especially) those who are not very bright, should not leave a class feeling stupid or inadequate. The old apprentice-master relationship was a formal one, a contract. There were rights and responsibilities in law on both sides. When a teacher became too old or ill to work, his graduates were meant to look after him.

Fosterage ended at maturity, when the youth returned to their birth family. Thus some other unfortunate had to cope with teenage tantrums, an arrangement that doubtless many modern parents might envy! An educational apprenticeship may have continued on beyond this age barrier.

Many people seem to have felt deeper bonds for their foster parents than for their biological family. Tradition has it that the festival of Lughnasadh was started as a commemoration of Lugh's own foster mother. The bond between apprentice and master may often have gone deep. The story of the young Fionn mac Cumhail gives us the example of the old Druid Finéces who asked the lad to cook the Salmon of Knowledge for him. Juices from the roasting fish splattered on to Fionn's fingers, and he put them in his mouth. Just as Gwion Bach unintentionally absorbed the magical power of the *Awen* in Welsh myth, so Fionn gained the knowledge of the salmon. Far from exploding in rage, old Finegas took this as an omen and instructed his pupil to eat the whole salmon, as the knowledge was destined to go to Fionn and not to the old man who has spent so long trying to catch the fish.

The pupil excels the master, and the master rejoices for him.

Some questions for you to think about:

- Do you think the old ideas about child rearing would work with modern children? Are those ideas better or worse than the way people treat their children these days?
- How do see the role of a teacher? How should a good teacher treat their pupils (does it make any difference if they are teaching children or adults)?
- How might a modern day Druid apply the idea of fosterage?

Practical exercise:

Plan a puberty ritual for a teen (an imaginary one, if there are no suitable real candidates around). Firstly, decide at which age this should be done ~ would it be on a specific birthday, or whenever puberty naturally occurs, or when some task has been accomplished etc. Secondly, decide who would be present ~ only people of the same gender, the whole family etc. Thirdly, consider what elements you would include (maybe read around the practices of other cultures for inspiration), for example....

- Special tasks ~ the Jewish bar mitzvah ceremony requires the boy to memorise a passage of the Torah and recite it for all those present.
- Seclusion ~ in Ghana young women go into a period of contemplation away from the rest of the tribe at their first menstruation.
- Change of name ~ as mentioned previously.
- Gifts ~ the Apache womanhood ceremony involves a presentation of gifts to the new woman.
- Decoration ~ the Congolese Pygmies paint special patterns on their skin during the ceremonies. Some other cultures have used permanent tattoos or scarification.
- Some cultures have engaged in activities that would be too

dangerous or even illegal in modern times, so there have to be limits! Fourthly, consider what you would educate the newly made adult about ~ what is the essence of manhood or womanhood? Finally, think about which deities you might call upon to guide the transition successfully.

Chapter Ten

Marriage and Gender

The early Irish had nine forms of marriage to choose between, whilst the Welsh had ten! These were mainly defined by which partner had the most money. The laws around marriage were called the *Cain Lánamna*, which also includes matters of divorce. *Lánamnas* is a word that originally meant a legally defined relationship between two unequal people, like a parent and child, or teacher and pupil. Eventually it was mostly used to describe a marriage.

The laws imply that the Irish saw marriage as mainly for child rearing. Being childless was grounds for divorce, and those types of relationships that did not produce kids did not require any kind of legal wedding service. For example, there are no surviving accounts of gay marriages, though there are suggestions of same-sex love surviving even the censorious Church scribes. These marital forms show some similarities to Roman law, which may have been either a direct influence or simply a parallel development.

Lánamnas comthichuir:	Both partners enter the union with equal financial resources.
Lánamnas mná for ferthinchur:	The man is the richer of the two partners.
Lánamnas fir for bantichur:	The woman is the richer.
Lánamnas fir thathigtheo:	The man visits the woman in her home with her family's consent, but does not live with her.
Lánamnas foxail:	The woman elopes openly with a man without the consent of her kin.

Lánamnas taidi:	The Soldier's Marriage (woman is secretly visited without knowledge of her kin).
Lánamnas eicne no sleithe:	The woman is forcibly raped or seduced by stealth.
Lánamnas fir mir:	Marriage of two "insane" persons.

The word *mir* used in the last type of marriage can describe anyone who was declared mentally incompetent, because they were insane, simple-minded, etc.

When a woman married each year her husband had to pay a sum of money called a *coibche*, the amount of which reflected her social status. In the first year this went to her family. In the second year most of it went to her family, but she kept a cut for herself. In the third year her cut got bigger, and so on until she kept the whole lot for herself. This was her cash to be spent on anything she chose. A husband had no rights over his wife's personal wealth (or vice versa). The humorous competition between Medb and her husband Aillil in the *Táin Bó Cúailnge* may be seen as a financial power-struggle, not just to brag about that had the most wealth but to see who had legal dominance within the relationship (and thus the kingdom).

If the couple divorced and the fault was on the man's side, the wife could keep all or most of her *coibche*. If the fault was on the woman's side, she had to pay back all or a large part of it to her husband.

To the modern mind, these assorted styles of marriage may seem terribly unromantic. The cheesy influence of Mills & Boon bodice rippers and Hollywood romance films pervades our culture, giving everyone the expectation of undying love, unending passion and all the rest of it. Which may go someway to explaining our divorce statistics, when the reality fails to live up to the fantasy. Whilst many modern people may not like the idea of fiscally based marriage contracts, the pragmatism that underlay the *Cáin Lánamnas* may well be something worth reflecting upon. Entering into a union with a clearer idea of who is responsible for providing what, might make disillusionment less likely.

The grounds for divorce varied between men and women. Women had more grounds for disposing of their husbands, and could also use the law to censure them for failing to do their "marital duty" ~

The husband who, through listlessness, does not go to his wife in her bed must pay a fine.

That law must have made for an entertaining court case! A woman's legal grounds for initiating divorce against her husband were as follows:

Her husband rejected her totally for another woman or a man,
the husband failed to support her financially,
the husband telling derogatory lies about or satirising her,
seducing her into marriage by trickery or sorcery,
the husband striking her hard enough to cause a blemish,
his impotence,
his being so grossly obese that sex became impossible,
his sterility,
his telling tales about their love life,
his joining a celibate Christian order.

A number of these grounds focus on the inability to breed. A man's reasons for divorce (which you can see were somewhat fewer) were:

Unfaithfulness,

persistent thievery,
self-inducing an abortion,
bringing shame to his honour,
smothering her child,
being without milk through illness.

It is curious that sterility was assumed to be a fault of the man, when in so many other cultures the woman has automatically carried the burden of blame. The issue of breast milk presumably only applied to marriages in the lower classes, where they could not afford to hire a wet nurse. As you can see one of the common themes here yet again is childlessness. A relationship that produced children ~ even if it were by rape or a one-night stand ~ required some sort of legal status to protect the child and to make one or both parents financially responsible. A relationship that did not produce children did not require legal protection, and so could be dissolved, in order to allow the parties to move on and find a relationship where children were a possibility.

However, the law must have recognised that love could override childlessness. It allowed for either spouse to enter into a legal contract with another party for the sake of pregnancy. So a woman with a sterile husband could arrange to sleep with another man in order to get pregnant. This would not constitute adultery, if done with formal approval of the law, and the resultant child could be classed as legally belonging to her husband rather than the biological father.

There is also evidence that at least a number of tribes allowed for polygyny (and some older evidence for polyandry too). Law commentaries from within the Christian period sought to justify this practice with reference to Old Testament practices ~ possibly it was such an ingrained hang-over from Pagan times that many people refused to give it up in favour of monogamy. One law makes it clear that men could have several wives ~

If the chief wife scratches the concubine but it is out of rightful jealousy that she does it, she is exempt from liability for injury. The same does not hold true for injuries by the concubine.

In some cultures there are very clearly defined expectations of how men and women should live and behave. Some jobs are considered suitable for women, others for men etc. It is very difficult to get a picture for how the early Celts viewed matters of gender. With jobs, for example, there does not appear to have been any barrier in either direction. Women could be Druids, judges, merchants etc. There do not appear to be records of any careers or daily activities from which men were excluded. This does not mean that women had total equality, or that getting into some professions was easy ~ just that it was possible. There may also have been differences between tribes as to what one regarded as manly/womanly and another did not.

Some cultures consider pretty clothes and cosmetics to be "girly". Yet there are numerous accounts of big beefy warriors primping and preening, and making a vain display of how handsome and well dressed they were. Many cultures see violence and courage as "laddish" traits, yet Celtic myth and history is full of warrior women behaving in very ferocious ways.

The qualities that were highly valued seem to have been valued in both sexes. Honesty, bravery, commitment to the tribe, generosity and being a good host were traits expected of everyone.

There are accounts of some single-sex situations. In legends told of the Irish adventurer Bran mac Febail, he and his fellows encounter an island called *Tir na mBan,* which is inhabited only by women. The *Fomóiri* giant Balor imprisoned his daughter Eithne on an island with only women for company, to prevent her getting pregnant (there being a prophecy that her future child would kill Balor). In late Welsh lore Arianrhod lived on an island where no men were allowed to live, perhaps an analogy to a convent or a distant memory of some older practice. In Celtic Christian tradition the Abbess Brigit founded a community for both nuns and monks, but there was an area in which a sacred flame was kept burning and into which no men were allowed to step foot. Indeed, it was said that a man who even peeked into the sanctuary would go blind. This was not in keeping with the practice of the wider Catholic Church at that time, so it could easily have been a practice carried over from Pagan times.

There do not seem to be any surviving stories about all-male islands or communities, but this does not mean that such things may not have existed. The reasons for why such communities may have formed in societies where gender-restricted behaviour seems irrelevant are unclear. Perhaps they did have ideas that there were certain things easier to achieve in a single-sex community than in a mixed one. It is unlikely to have been out of a desire to encourage celibacy. Early Christian nuns and monks could marry and have children. It was only at the insistence of the Vatican that the clergy eventually became celibate. There does not appear to have been any strident restrictions against men having sex with each other, or women doing likewise. The great hero Cú Chulainn maintained a very intimate relationship with the warrior Ferdiad, and sang love songs praising his manly beauty over the corpse. Not proof that they were lovers, but certainly suggestive. Such relationships appeared to have no stigma about them, so people in single-sex religious communities are unlikely to have been bereft of offers!

It is possible that single-sex communities may have been composed of people who only wanted sex with their own gender, but when the adventurer Bran mac Febail arrived on an island of women, he and his male colleagues were welcomed with open arms. It seems unlikely that these were communities of early lesbian separatists, at least in the minds of the scribes! It may be that such groups formed because of beliefs around certain types of magic, either in the view that some forms of magical energy were more easily raised in an all-female (or all-male) environment, or because the magic was directed towards some goal that was only of interest to one gender. Unless a long-lost text turns up to answer these questions, we will never really know for sure.

Some questions for you to think about:

- How do you view gender in the modern world ~ what do you consider proper masculine or feminine behaviour?
- Are there any insights into modern relationships that we could gain from studying the marriage and divorce laws of the Brehons?
- What are some of the advantages of single-sex communities? Have you ever participated in a single-sex ritual? If so, how do you feel it differed from a ritual with both men and women present?

Practical exercise:

Organise an activity with a group of friends the same gender as yourself ~ it doesn't have to be anything particularly Druidic, it could be a night on the town, walk in the woods, a sporting event, etc.

Use the opportunity to watch how a group of men (or women) interact with each other ~ is it significantly different from when they interact in a mixed setting? Reflect on how you feel when with your own gender. Is gender a stronger indicator of behaviour than social class, religion, sexuality, etc? Keep a log of your observations and reactions, for future reflection.

Chapter Eleven

Creating Healthy Communities

These days the various generations of a family tend to live far apart. Many children may only see their grandparents or aunts and uncles at holidays, if even then. In ancient times tribes were far more close-knit. Whilst some relatives may have been off at war, on mercantile trips, at sea etc, the majority of families would have lived cheek by jowl. An average-sized roundhouse might have contained three or more generations of the same family, including aunts, uncles etc.

Though obviously no statistics have survived, it is most likely that infant mortality was high, as it is in most rural societies living without all our modern technology. Female mortality, during childbirth, is also likely to have been fairly high. So only a comparatively small number of people would have made it to old age. There is, however, a fair amount of evidence to suggest that the elderly were well regarded by the younger generations. The modern habit of dumping granny in an Old Folks Home was unknown back then.

The Brehon laws required a certain degree of basic care, even specifying the minimum number of times that elderly relatives should be provided with baths and other essential needs. The minimum requirement towards a geriatric relative was ~

When you become old your family must provide you with one oatcake a day, plus a container of sour milk. They must bathe you every twentieth night and wash your head every Saturday. Seventeen sticks of firewood is the allotment for keeping you warm.

Most elderly relatives would have lived with their wider families, and so would not have required separate feeding or firewood.

This law was largely for those few people who lived by themselves, and had relatives visit them. Clearly the provision of one oatcake a day was in addition to whatever food they provided for themselves (otherwise they would have starved to death if that was their sole daily intake!).

Many modern Pagan books, particularly those with a Wiccan bent, often feature a Croning Ritual to mark a woman's transition through the menopause. Plenty also add an Elderhood Ritual for men of a similar age. There are no surviving records of what the ancient Celts did (if they did anything at all) at this stage in a person's life. There may have been elaborate rites, or a simple feast to mark the event, though it's possible that some tribes may not have considered it particularly important. We just don't know. However, there is nothing to stop modern day Druids from inventing their own ritual to mark entry into elderhood. There is a goddess popular throughout the Gaelic-speaking countries called the Cailleach, whose name translates as 'Old Woman' or 'Veiled One'. She is a goddess powerful enough to shape mountains and transform summer into winter, which suggests the elderly were not conceived of as ineffectual or relegated to powerless roles in ancient society.

Those whose frailty prevented them from contributing much physically would still have been turned to as sources of great wisdom, having had a lifetime of exercising their talents and acquiring knowledge. Their knowledge could still help to shape the world around them.

The law also expected people to exercise a duty of care towards each other, regardless of age. A person who witnessed a crime taking place and did not try to stop it or help in anyway could be charged with *forcsiu*, which meant 'over-looking' ~ in other words, standing round and doing bugger all. This same law was applied to people who gave shelter or support to runaway criminals. Over-looking is also referred to as one of the five-fold crimes (more on this in a subsequent chapter), namely:

The crime of the eye, by watching while an evil deed is taking place.
Tolerance of somebody else's crime was considered socially
irresponsible, and reflects the early Irish (and presumably British)
view that justice in the widest sense was something everyone had
to make happen ~ or be held accountable for not doing so.

People who were found guilty of GBH were required to pay
othrus ~ which means sick maintenance. Until their victim
recovered from their injuries, the attacker had to pay money
towards the medical bills and compensate for lost earnings. If the
injury caused a permanent disability, then the attacker would
have to pay *crólige bais*, an on-going financial support that would
last for the remainder of the victim's life. Cynics have suggested
that it would have been cheaper just to polish the victim off
entirely, and indeed some attackers may have taken just that
approach!

Each tribal chieftain had a legal duty to collect sufficient tax
money to pay for a public hospital, known as a *tigh-eiridinn*, or
House of Nursing. This was probably the earliest recorded form
of National Health Service. Everyone in a tribe was entitled to a
free minimum level of medical care, in exchange for having paid
their taxes. The old laws were quite specific about how these
hospitals were to be run ~ and include a lot of ideas that have only
recently been reintroduced. The laws stated that hospitals should
be well ventilated; should have clean running water; should be
kept clean and tidy at all times; that visitors should behave calmly
and quietly. An example of a law relating to doctors runs:

*The doctor shall build his house over a running stream. His house
must not be slovenly or smeared with the tracks of snails. It must
have four doors that open out so the patients may be seen from every
side at all times.*

The importance of some buildings having multiple doors recurs
in a number of myths, such as Da Derga's hostel having seven

doors (that number again!) It may be that there was some metaphysical symbolism underlying the need for many entrances, as well as the apparent practical reason of visitors being able to see in that is given in the quote. After Christianity became dominant in Britain, many people believed that washing too often was unnatural and dangerous. Whilst several Welsh saints were considered a little obsessive with their urge to stand in rivers, other holy men ~ perhaps most notable Martin of Tours, who destroyed many Pagan shrines in Gaul including an attempt on a sacred pine tree ~ were so pungent that even fellow religious avoided them! Several influential saints considered bathing to be a form of vanity, and so sinful. Queen Elizabeth I notoriously only took one bath a month, and was considered very fastidious for doing it as often as she did.

Florence Nightingale had to campaign for years to encourage hospitals to have trained nurses, rather than underpaid drunks to look after the patients. It took ages for her to convince doctors that opening the windows to let in fresh air was actually good for people.

The extent of medical knowledge amongst the old tribes is still being discovered. Recent archaeological discoveries in Colchester revealed a set of surgical tools whose design was so good that their modern counterparts have hardly changed at all.

There are legends of surgical achievements, such as when Nuada lost his hand in battle and the god Dian Cecht made him an artificial arm of silver. Later the god's son, Miach, found a way to re-attach the original severed limb. Miach also implanted a cat's eye into the empty socket of a man who had lost an eye ~ with rather bizarre results. Outside of the highly entertaining realms of Dr Who, it seems profoundly unlikely that the old tribes would have had the technology to actually carry out limb re-attachment, cybernetics or cross-species implants. However, the fact that they could dream up the possibility of doing it many centuries before such things were even remotely possible is, in itself, intriguing.

As well as curing illness, the old tribes made moves towards what these days is called 'social inclusion' ~ ensuring that people with medical problems were included in society, and given the means to contribute, rather than just being dumped in a corner. One example of this is Hand Ogam, a system for communicating with mute people. Various points on the hand represent different letters and, by touching parts of the hand, messages can be spelt out. In a tribal society, where food may often have been quite scarce, it was important that everyone be encouraged to contribute as much as they could. Such societies could not afford to carry people who did not contribute, whether due to illness or selfishness. In the latter case, lazy or selfish people were considered fair game. One law stated:

The selfish man, who thinks only of his cows and his fields, and not of his fellow human beings, may be insulted without risking a blush fine.

The Celtic response to illness and disability was an ambiguous one. The rules about who could become and remain a chieftain were very strict, and any kind of physical blemish could disbar someone from office. This included things that would seem fairly trivial by modern standards. One myth recounts how a very bad king, Bres, was cursed by a poet he had mistreated. The curse caused Bres to erupt in boils all over his body, which was enough for him to be legally forced to abdicate. When Nuada, one of the chieftains of the *Tuatha Dé Danann*, lost his hand in battle, he was also forced to pass on the throne to another.

The laws prohibiting disfigured or disabled people from office seem to have applied almost entirely to the role of *Rí*, or monarch. The most likely origin of this was the requirement that chieftains lead their warriors into battle ~ a task that would clearly have been risky for the blind or one-legged! The extension of this need for health may have developed to include a bar against people with skin complaints and other minor ailments for all sorts of reasons, some sensible and some not. There are several accounts of blind bards, so clearly these sorts of medical conditions were not considered a bar to religious vocations.

Various laws existed to protect people who, in this modern age, would be classed as having a mental illness or being mentally disabled. It was even considered illegal to take the piss out of someone because of his or her disability. Taunting someone could result in a fine. Some historians have tried to portray the ancient Insular Celts as a brutal warrior society, full of blood-crazed thugs who slit the throats of the weak and dependent. Hopefully this lesson has shown that this was simply not true. Far from being a bunch of intolerant yobs, the ancient tribes bent over backwards to provide support and care for the sick, the frail and the disabled.

Moving into a modern context, one might ponder how these ancient examples could inspire the 21st century Druid. The role of the polytheist religions has changed dramatically; where they were once the bedrock of mainstream society, now they are the preserve of the peculiar! Many people come to the Pagan faiths after being disillusioned by whichever mainstream religion or thought-system they grew up in. The word religion stems from a Latin root that meant to bond, tie or link. In theory a Pagan religion like Druidry should connect the individual to the world around them ~ not just the world of forests and fields, but of the village or city too. Many people relish the atmosphere of being in some sort of secretive spiritual clique, and pull their robes about them like a suit of armour shielding them from the Big Bad World. Ideally Druidry would inspire its adherents with ways in which to make the world better for all concerned, and the confidence to take their place within Society ~ not as laughable eccentrics, but as movers and shakers, philanthropists and visionaries.

If Druidry stirs your soul, try to view the sacred grove as a place to plan and prepare, rather than as a retreat to shelter from a cruel or frightening world of which you want no part.

Some questions for you to think about:

- Which people in your life have a duty towards you? This might be a family member, people whose work requires them to do certain things for you, friends, or anyone at all. Can you think of examples of what sort of duties are owed towards you?
- To whom do you have a duty? As above, it could be all sorts of people, or pets, places, precious objects you have a care for etc.
- What steps could Society take towards changing the behaviour of those who fail to meet their duties?

Practical Exercise:

If you do not already do so, spend some time helping out a frail or unwell relative, friend or (if that is not an option) stranger via a charity. What you do is up to you ~ anything from just spending time with them, to doing their shopping or gardening or more personal care. The amount of time you spend is, again, down to you. It could be just the odd hour, or you might decide to make this an ongoing commitment.

If you are too frail/unwell yourself to help another, then spend the time trying to deepen the relationship with whoever provides you with care ~ get to know more about them, their opinions, life experiences, hopes, fears etc.

Further, contemplate ways in which you could get involved in civic affairs. It may be something discreet like tree-planting or litter-picking schemes; it could be attending an Interfaith group to learn about other people and teach them about Druidry; it could be some higher profile work, representing your local Pagan community at civic functions. Whatever line you take, the important aspect is that you become involved with the wider community within which you live.

Chapter Twelve

Funeral Rites and the Afterlife

The assorted Irish and British tribes used a wide variety of different funeral rites, and often the same tribe would change methods several times over the course of the centuries. To cover every piece of archaeological evidence would take far too long, so we will concentrate on just a few examples of different ways in which the old tribes disposed of their dead.

Burials were common. Some tribes made huge mounds in which a great many people were interred ~ they must have had operable doorways at some point to allow new corpses to be added. Several of the British burial mounds continued to be used well into the Anglo-Saxon period. Other tribes placed bodies in individual graves. Most tribes seem to have included grave goods. Some of these items were things that the dead probably used in life, others seem to have been protective amulets, yet others seem to be items made especially for the dead (this can be discerned because some things are made in such a way that they would fall apart if used by the living). An example of the latter is the case of a pair of shoes covered in fragile gold leaf ~ no good for actually walking, at least not for walking in this world!

Cremations were quite popular at certain points in time. One widespread practice was to burn the body on a pyre of wood (maybe with grave goods ~ it's hard to know, given that they would be reduced to ashes), and then scoop up the ashes once cool, tip them into a large jar, and bury the jar. Julius Caesar reported on the funeral rites of the Gauls (presumably the upper class ones), saying:

Their funerals, considering the state of civilisation amongst the Gauls, are magnificent and costly; and they cast into the fire all

things, including living creatures, which they suppose to have been
dear to them when alive; and, a little before this period, slaves and
dependents, who were ascertained to have been beloved by them,
were, after the regular funeral rites were completed, burnt together
with them.

As mentioned earlier, there is plenty of evidence for goods placed in graves and mounds for interment funerals. So it's not unreasonable to suppose that some tribes may have made burnt offerings as well. Had people been thrown on to the funeral pyres on a regular basis, then we would expect some evidence in terms of additional charred bones etc. So far no real evidence of this has transpired. There are no references from other contemporary writers, or in myths, to back up the idea that chucking relatives and servants on funeral pyres was widespread. For a while the Egyptians used to entomb servants with pharaohs, but soon stopped this when it became obvious how wasteful it was. Incinerating servants or widows may have been a (hopefully brief) fad amongst certain Gallic tribes, or it may be that Caesar had misunderstood something that he had heard about second-hand.

Some tribes used exposure. This would have involved putting a corpse out in the open air, most likely on top of a high wooden platform. The birds and bugs would eventually strip the bones clean, whereupon they would be gathered up and then buried. Sometimes the bones were interred in their own private hole, sometimes gathered together in a large mound along with the bones of many other people. One Scottish tribe used the waters of a peat bog to preserve two corpses, which were then propped up in a hut and stayed there in a mummified state for several centuries before being buried. Some Andean tribes kept wind-dried corpses of tribal elders in huts, in order to commune with them. Probably something similar happened with the northern tribe.

No outright descriptions of the soul's passage beyond the grave have survived for modern Druids, the way it has for followers of the Egyptian religion. However, by reading the various myths and accounts, certain features of the Afterlife as the old tribes saw it may be guessed at. Whether the modern Druid agrees completely with the old tribes on these matters, or follows their own vision, is entirely up to them.

The Irish myths talk of Donn as being the Lord of the Dead, and an island off the coast of Munster near to Dursey Island is called Tech Duinn ~ the House of Donn. Folklore has it that this is where the souls of those dying in Ireland go. Whether they stay there, or if it is more like a waiting room for the next phase, is unclear. Donn was the first member of the *Milesians* to die ~ in one version of the legend he fell overboard and drowned even before the ship could land. He was buried on Tech Duinn. Many scholars have argued that Donn is actually a much older god who predates the story of the Coming of Mil. An account of this drowning story in the medieval *'Historia Brittonum'* credits Donn with the memorable phrase: *'To me, to my house, come you all after death.'* This quote can often be heard spoken at modern Druid funerals.

When writing about the Gallic tribes he had been warring against, Julius Caesar wrote:

All the Gauls assert that they are descended from the god Dis, and say that this tradition has been handed down by the Druids.

Dis Pater was the Roman god of death and the underworld, and Caesar clearly had reason to believe that the Gauls considered themselves to be descended from a god of the dead very similar in character or function to the Roman deity. We do not know with any degree of certainty what god the Gauls associated with the dead, but perhaps it was one very similar in nature to Donn. Whilst no myth has survived, it may well be that the Irish considered themselves descendants of Donn or a deity very much like him. Some scholars have speculated that Caesar may have been referring to Cernunnos when he talked about Dis Pater.

Irish traditions tend to envision the Afterlife as being entered through a location that is almost always off to the west (where the sun sets) and usually either an island at sea or a place actually under the water, or within a hill.

The Welsh legends do not specify that *Annwn* is the land of the dead (it is just described as a magical, Otherworldly place), but many modern Pagans see it as such. This place is ruled over by a number of chieftains, the most prominent of who is Arawn the huntsman. *Annwn* is described as a place full of feasting, fighting, rejoicing etc. The hero Pwyll journeyed there and spent a year in the court of Arawn doing most of the same things he would have been doing at his own court in Wales. The Afterlife was often seen as not much different from the current life, though perhaps with more fun and adventure (and a few strange creatures thrown in for good measure).

Whilst the Irish associated the entry to the Afterlife with places at sea, the Welsh tended to think of *Annwn* (assuming the modern Pagan view that this is the place of the dead is correct) as being underground. There are numerous references to the dead (especially heroes) sleeping in hollow hills, waiting for the call to return to life; the most famous being King Arthur.

One account speaks of Druids laughing at funerals and crying at baptisms. The reason given was that, at a funeral the soul was reborn into the Afterlife and so the Druids rejoiced at this. At baptisms it was regarded that the baby must have died in the Otherworld in order to be born into this world, and so the Druids wept to mourn its passing from the spirit world.

The image this conveys is of two (at least) worlds, this one and the Otherworld. The soul is born here, inhabits a body and does all the usual things. At some point the body dies, and the soul moves to the Otherworld and inhabits a body there and does whatever it is that people do in that place (myth suggests that it's not much different from what people do here).

Caesar said that the belief in reincarnation was so strong that warriors went fearless into battle, convinced that if they died with honour then they would be reborn into an honourable life elsewhere.

They wish to inculcate this as one of their leading tenets, that souls do not become extinct, but pass after death from one body to another, and they think that men by this tenet are in a great degree excited to valour, the fear of death being disregarded.

The Greek writer Polyhistor added a commonly held view about the link between Druidic and Pythagorean thought, when he wrote:

The Pythagorean doctrine prevails among the Gauls' teaching that the souls of men are immortal, and that after a fixed number of years they will enter into another body.

Both these quotes seem to support the idea of some style of reincarnation. Polyhistor's writings pose the question as to what the soul was believed to do during that period of fixed years betwixt bodies. Possibly the soul may have resided in some Otherworldly location?

Many myths contain accounts of people transforming into a whole series of different animals, often before being reborn as another human being. Tuan mac Cairill, for example, dwelt first as a human, then 300 years each as a stag, boar, eagle and salmon, before becoming human again. Assorted similar stories reinforce this claim that Druids believed in transmigration ~ the ability to come back in non-human form. Some Eastern religions feel that people reincarnate as animals if they have failed to learn certain lessons as humans. There is no suggestion of this in Celtic myth, and the soul's lives in animal form are often filled with magical powers and great insight. Some modern Pagans believe that the soul does not reincarnate as such, but the spirit energy is recycled in much the same way as the corpse is, and continues on as part of the universal pattern.

The early text called *'Conversation of Colum Cille with the Youth at Carn Eolairg'* (which dates back to the 8th, possibly 7th century dual-faith period) has an unnamed youth describing a lake that covers the site of a lost land, which may possibly be *Mag Fuinsidi* (a name given in a related poem).

I have grazed it when I was a stag; I have swum it when I was a salmon, when I was seal; I have run upon it when I was a wolf; I have gone around it when I was a human.

It is very easy to read a doctrine of transmigration into this story. The strange young man goes on to say,

I have landed there [the sunken kingdom] *under three sails: the yellow sail which bears, the green sail which drowns, the red sail under which bodies were conceived.*

This could be taken to suggest stages of life from birth to death to conception again ~ in other words, reincarnation. The youth had lived, died and been reborn in the now lost land. The symbolism of the colours might stem from Pagan traditions known to the scribe. Green seems an odd choice for death, given that most people today would be more likely to conceive of it as a colour more associated with life and verdant growth ~ unless, perhaps, the emphasis is on death by drowning rather than death per se. In Norse myth those who drown have a special Afterlife reserved for them in the halls of the goddess Ran, so there is a slim possibility the colour may have been linked to a watery Irish deity with guardianship over the drowned[26]. As has already been mentioned, the land of the dead is often associated with under-water regions in Irish lore and a deity of the dead may well also have been associated with fresh or salt water.

Some cultures associate a particular colour with death, and may incorporate it into funeral attire, winding sheets, flowers and the like. There is no evidence from excavated graves of a specific colour theme, though it is really only speculative that the imagery of the *"green sail"* might have carried over into funeral behaviour. Though there is no evidence for usage outside this symbolic, lyrical writing, a modern Druid might find the use of colour inspirational and apply it in various ways to rites for death, conception, or birth.

Valerius Maximus, an early writer from 25CE, noted that the Celtic belief in the Otherworld was so strong that there was a tradition of being able to repay a debt in the afterlife. A person's debts did not transfer to their children.

For it is said that they lend to each other sums that are repayable in the next world, so firmly convinced are they that the souls of men are immortal.

The Irish monk now nicknamed Augustine Hibernicus (his real name is unknown) wrote an interesting treatise[27] on the nature of miracles, sometime around 655CE. In it he scorned the beliefs of his forebears, which appear to indicate a belief in the dead becoming birds. The more famous Saint Augustine of Hippo, with whom this scribe was initially confused, also criticised the supposedly too-radical Pelagian[28] heretics for espousing a similar belief in bird-souls.

[S]how assent to the ridiculous myths of the magicians who say that their ancestors flew through the ages in the form of birds.

The word *magorum* is translated here as magicians, and refers to the Irish Magi, in other words Druids. What is not clear is if these *magorum* believed that the deceased soul assumed a magical avian form, a belief also found in Ancient Egypt where the *Ka* was often depicted in winged form, or if they regarded sparrows, eagles etc as reincarnated humans. Given that this manuscript was written in 655CE when there were still a fair few Pagans about, the anonymous monk may well have met some and heard their views firsthand.

Another monastic, contained in the Book of Armagh, raises some ~ though yet again frustratingly vague ~ intriguing possibilities. The author of the *Collectanea* section, Tírechán (mentioned in a previous chapter), contains a rebuttal to St Patrick's offer of baptism supposedly made by the aristocrat Loegaire. He describes how his father, King Niall, had insisted that he remain Pagan in order to be buried at the royal seat of Tara.

> *for the Pagans, armed in their tombs, bear weapons at the ready – face to face until the day of erdathe – as the Druids say; that is, the day of the Lord's judgement.*

The burial of warriors with their weapons is an attested fact, though this passage gives the added prospect that these weapons are not merely there out of some sort of militaristic nostalgia but are *'at the ready'*, i.e. expected to be used in a future battle. It almost seems to suggest a bodily resurrection, in which the restored corpse will have its grave goods to hand. Christianity at that point, and for a long time afterwards, held to a doctrine of physical resurrection. Tírechán may have transposed his own beliefs onto this ancient warrior, or he may have recorded a Pagan belief genuinely held, at least within that tribe if not all others. The day of *erdathe* is a decided curiosity. The scribe compares it to Judgement Day, and it may possibly have been just that ~ a time when the Gods assessed the dead (whether each person faced their own individual judgement, or if there was a mass event for all the dead is unclear).

John Carey (1996[29]) considered this quote in conjunction with another from the same manuscript, drawing comparison with the Germanic concept of Ragnarok. Historians and Heathen scholars alike continue to debate if Ragnarok itself is a genuine ancient Germanic polytheist belief, or an attempt by later Christian writers to integrate a parallel to Armageddon into their sagas. If we momentarily assume that Ragnarok is a genuinely Heathen notion, then possibly other Northern European tribes also had an idea of some cataclysmic battle prophesied to take place in a distant future, and for which fierce warriors would be needed to leap fully armed from their graves. Ragnarok is fought between Gods and Giants, an easy parallel to which can be found in the medieval manuscripts ~ the *Tuatha Dé* and the *Fomóiri*, though this is presented as a past event rather than a prophecy of a future one.

The secondary quote deals with St Patrick's arrival at a Pagan healing well in Connaught called *Slán* of which the manuscript says:

> *the Druids honoured that spring and sacrificed gifts to it as if it were a god. It was a four-sided spring, and there was a four-sided stone in the spring's mouth [...] the unbelievers said that a certain deceased prophet made a casket for himself in the water beneath the stone, so that his bones could whiten forever, for he feared the burning of fire.*

The identity of the dead prophet is unknown, but the scenario echoes numerous tales of lakes bursting out over the graves of assorted legendary characters after whom they are then named. The making of offerings to sacred lakes is an accepted aspect of early Celtic ritual practice, and it may be wondered if the reasoning behind many such offerings was the knowledge (or belief) that some ancient worthy was buried beneath the waters. Four-sided pillars crop up in a number of legendary contexts, probably attempts at accounting for all those ancient dressed menhirs.

For Carey the juxtaposition of water and fire in this 7th century Irish tale echoes all the way back to Strabo's claim that the Gallic Druids,

say that souls and the cosmos are indestructible, but that sometimes fire and water will overpower them.

The Greek quote implies that conflagration and flood are equally dangerous, whilst the Irish prophet (whom one assumes to have been a Druid) seems to have been sheltering in one element to avoid the other. In this respect the Tírechán quote perhaps has more in common with another story of his, that St Patrick struck a bargain with the Christian god that the Irish should be spared whatever terrible (and possibly fiery) fate awaits the rest of humanity on Judgement Day. Seven years prior to the last act, Ireland would be flooded. If the Irish were all drowned, this scarcely seems a better fate, but perhaps the feeling was more that they would rest serenely on the ocean floor until the waters receded and they could arise anew?

Carey suggests that the hagiographic tale may have evolved out of a missionary ploy to convert the 'unbelievers'. If the old Druids did indeed have a prophecy that some terrible event (a wrathful judgement, a vast war etc) would one day befall the world, then the missionaries may have decided not to dismiss it as nonsense but accept it as real ~ with the added proviso that Christ would offer a way of avoiding the calamity, and that this would (for whatever reason) involve hiding in water. The latter may have been an innovation on the part of missionaries, or perhaps they replaced some pre-existing saviour figure (possibly some sort of river- or ocean-deity) with Jesus.

If *erdathe* might contain echoes of Ragnarok, then the assorted mentions of flame and water remind this author of the two major elements of Germanic cosmology: fire and ice. Heathen myths tell of the cosmos being created from the interaction of frosty Niflheim and sweltering Muspelheim. As ever it is merely speculation, but perhaps the Celts saw their universe as being generated by the tensions between forces of water and fire. One could go off at a tangent and get positively Taoist, seeing an admonishment to balance in the rebuke supposedly made by Druids about Patrick saying,

> *by turns, in alternate years, this man reveres now water and now fire as a god.*

To return to the unnamed prophet beneath the well, his alleged concern for the survival of his bones seems to imply that the state of ones mortal remains was seen as having a long-term significance. What did he believe would happen to his soul if his bones were eventually incinerated in some future doomsday scenario?

The previous quote from Strabo emphasised that the world was indestructible, that it would survive any terrible disasters much as the Earth actually survives Ragnarok along with the best of the Aesir and Vanir. The apocalypse is more a purification than a termination.

The *fled co-lige* was a feast given to honour the dead, and is probably the origin of the Irish wake. The much later Welsh Christian tradition of the sin-eater, an outcast who consumed the sins of the deceased by eating a meal (sometimes from a plate placed on the coffin) on behalf of the deceased, may also stem from this practice. Feasting was a major feature of funerals, including food for the dead. It was very common to place offerings of meat, beer, mead etc in the grave or burial mound. Strabo claimed that the ancient Irish actually ate their own dead, but there is no evidence for cannibalism on that scale. After the feast they held the *cluiche caintech*, or funeral games. There do not appear to be any strong indications as to which games, but we know that Lughnasadh ~ itself traditionally a festival inaugurated to mark the death of the goddess Tailtiu ~ was marked by lots of horse racing, athletics displays and similar sporting events. So possibly the funeral games went along the same lines. Either they were the deceased's favourite sports, or perhaps some game that symbolised the soul's journey.

Whilst on the topic of Tailtiu it is worth pausing awhile to contemplate the nature of non-human life and death. Numerous cultures have tales of deities who die (Baldr and Tammuz to name but two). How are polytheists to understand this, in what meaningful sense can a deity be said to be dead? There is an obvious degree of nature symbolism in Tailtiu's story, with the land giving its all in harvest and then falling into an exhausted and deathly slumber over winter. Possibly death could be seen as a metaphor for a period when a deity is, at least as far as humans are concerned, dormant. Ought a polytheist Druid then try to contact Tailtiu during the winter season, or is she to be considered symbolically dead and in some manner incommunicado during the post-Lughnasadh period?

As well as musing on the nature of what death might mean for a theoretically immortal being, we may also contemplate the concept of death in an animist universe. If rocks and rivers and swords have living souls that sporadically communicate with passing Druids, can they then die? If they can die, how would one tell if a rock is dead or alive (and what kills it ~ a good thwack with a hammer)? If such bizarre conundrums ever get answered, we might then move on to contemplate what the Afterlife holds for a dead river nymph.

At one point a *filid* or bard would make a requiem song, called an *ecnaire* in Gaelic or a *cerdd farwnad* in Welsh; then would follow the elegy, a poem praising the deceased's life, called a *nuall-guba*. The recitation of poetry was standard for the rich ~ whether peasants also received such fancy funeral rites, we do not know. Families too poor to hire a fancy bard may well have composed their own elegies. The actual interment was attended with a chorus of people wailing and keening (from the Irish *caoine*) and rhythmically clapping their hands (*lamh-comairt*), probably in tune with a slow drumbeat. This seems to have been the only sombre moment in the ceremony, and was probably a good release valve for the pent-up grief of the widowed or orphaned. Some sources talk about the graves being marked by stones or wooden posts inscribed with ogam ~ presumably the name of the corpse. There is a popular tradition still of mourners visiting a grave to leave a small pebble. In time ~ at least if the deceased were popular enough to have many visits ~ those stones could build up into quite a mound, called a *cairn* or a *barp*.

Some questions for you to think about:

- What would you like to leave behind when you shuffle off this mortal coil and become an ex-Druid? Reflect on your hoped-for legacy, both in terms of the achievements and impact on other people, and also of the material goods ~ what do you wish to happen to any Pagan goodies in your possession (swords, books, wands, crystal balls etc)?

- What do you feel the Afterlife is like, if you believe in one at all? Do you think all people go to the same place, or are there different afterlives for different people (according to religion, or how they lived their life etc)?

- Speaking of which, how does ones life influence ones Afterlife? Does a paedophile find the same Otherworld waiting for them as a surgeon who has saved thousands of lives? Is there any sense of reward or punishment in the world beyond?

Practical exercise:

A codicil can be added to your will, describing the type of funeral you want. So long as your wishes are within the law, the codicil then becomes legally enforceable by whoever you have appointed to organise the event. Plan your own funeral, if you have not already done so. Think about the following issues ~

- Burial, cremation, exposure etc. What would you prefer?
- Do you want a fancy coffin, a plain box, a cardboard coffin, a wicket basket, just a winding sheet?
- What should your corpse be dressed in... a suit/nice frock, Druid robes, a pink tutu, biker leathers etc?
- Are there any grave goods you want placed in your coffin, or added to your funeral pyre?
- What music would you like played at the ceremony?
- Have you a favourite piece of poetry that you would like to be read out (and who do you want to read it)?
- Wreaths, flowers, donations to a charity, or something else?
- How should the mourners dress... all in black, in fancy dress, in rainbow hues etc?
- Do you want a Wake of some description? Open to all and sundry, or just a chosen few.

Chapter Thirteen

Animals in Society and Religion

The old tribes lived alongside their animals in a way that few people in modern industrialised societies do. People would often sleep in sectioned-off areas whilst their farm animals slept in the main body of the house. Not just dogs, but sheep cows, goats etc. Animals were not only a source of food, but also of wool, leather, fertiliser, bone, hides, glue and so forth. Some animals were status symbols.

Cattle were a mobile form of wealth, and the larger ones herd the higher ones social standing. Horses and hunting hounds were popular gifts to be given by chieftains to their loyal warriors.

In addition to farm animals, there are references to the insular tribes having kept pets. Caesar talked about chickens and hares being popular, and there are assorted accounts of both people and Gods having lap dogs and cats. Lugh has a pet dog called Failinis, who radiates enough light to blind an enemy and was acquired for him by the Children of Tuireann. The warrior-poet Caoilte said of the magical bitch that she was:

> *That hound of mightiest deeds,*
> *Which was irresistible in hardness of combat,*
> *Was better than wealth ever known,*
> *A ball of fire every night.*

> *Other virtues had that beautiful hound*
> *(Better this property than any other property),*
> *Mead or wine would grow of it,*
> *Should it bathe in spring water.*

Queen Medb of the Connacht had a pet bird (species unspecified) and a red squirrel, which sat on her shoulder, as described in the *Táin Bó Cúailnge*:

> *Medb passed over the ford eastwards, and again he cast a stone from his sling at her east of the ford, so that it killed the tame squirrel that was on her shoulder.*

The sorts of wild animals that appear most prominently in myths are those that were hunted for meat, pelts etc. Most of these species are now extinct in Britain and Ireland, save for a few creatures in zoos. Wild bears and wolves are all now extinct in Britain. Wild pigs (reintroduced from the continent) are being farmed, and some have escaped from farms and bred in small sounders in the woods, along with the reintroduced beavers. One millionaire landowner in Scotland wants to reintroduce wolves on his estate.

Those few statues of Gods and Goddesses that have survived from the Iron Age almost always shows them either accompanied by animals, or having certain animal features ~ such as antlers, and tails etc. Quite a few of the Pictish standing stones have beautiful carvings of animals on them, including some creatures that are mythical (such as axe-wielding centaurs and bird-headed men) and some that are so stylised as to be hard to identify. The so-called cetus creatures may possibly be dolphins, but no-one is really sure.

We know that a certain amount of animal sacrifice went on, though it must be born in mind that animals killed for ritual would invariably be eaten in the great feast that concluded the ceremony. They weren't just left on altars to rot. Meat was often put into graves, so the dead could feast in the Otherworld.

The ritual of *tarb-feis*, when a bull was killed and the meat cooked up whilst a Druid went into trance, involved the idea of consuming a sacred animal in order to partake of its magical powers. The *imbas forosnai* spell also involved eating a sacred animal as part of entering a trance and gaining advice from its spirit. The idea of eating something to become part of it is ancient and almost global in spread. One can even see this idea in Catholicism, with the consumption of Jesus via the wine and wafer.

Shape-shifting is a recurrent theme in Cetic myth. Sometimes this happens willingly, as when Cian turned himself into a pig to escape his enemies. Sometimes it is unwontedly visited upon a person, as when the wizard Gwydion was turned into a wolf by his uncle's spell. Whether our distant ancestors believed people could physically change shape (as the myths suggest), or whether they saw it as a more spiritual, trance-induced psychological transformation (as most modern people regard it), we do not know.

Animals appear not only in terms of marking change within a person, but also within time. Historians the world over use metaphors to describe periods of time. Modern historians talk about the Stone Age, Bronze Age etc. Greek myth speaks of the Golden Age, Silver Age and so forth. Hesiod used a similar pattern to the ones given below for measuring the somewhat fanciful age of the world. In China people have the Year of the Ox, Year of the Dragon etc. We have what might be a hint of this sort of thing from native sources. The Scots Gaelic 'Book of the Dean of Lismore', composed in the early 1400's, contains the following verse:

> *Three life-times of the Stag for the Blackbird,*
> *Three life-times of the Blackbird for the Eagle,*
> *Three life-times of the Eagle for the Salmon,*
> *Three life-times of the Salmon for the Yew.*

This quote is not meant to be taken as a literal comment that people back then thought blackbirds lived much longer than deer. Rather, these could be legendary periods of time. The Book was penned some 700-odd years after the influence of the Druids had dwindled into insignificance, so it is unlikely to have been used in a Pagan context. However, it is not unknown for colloquialisms and phrases to be used long after their original context has been forgotten (and yes, I know I'm stretching this a bit, but I just adore animal imagery!). The quote brings to mind the stories of Tuan mac Cairill and Fintan, both of whom spent long periods of time in the shape of different animals, watching and recording momentous events. We no longer know for sure, but it's possible that the old tribes measured time using animal metaphors. Whilst people were not doing this in the 15th century, the passage might possibly (can you hear the elastic stretching yet?) be a distant echo of a time when people might have spoken of the Age of the Stag, the Century of the Eagle etc.

In the Welsh story where the hero Culhwch was hunting for a lost child, he was passed from one ancient animal to another ~ each one saying that they had not seen the child but the next older creature might have. There is another traditional verse that runs:

A year for a stalk, three years for a garden,
Thrice the age of a garden for a hound,
Thrice the age of a hound for a horse
Thrice the age of a horse for a man,
Thrice the age of a man for a wild deer,
Thrice the age of a wild deer for a blackbird.

Again this does not seem meant to be taken as zoological fact. Any tribe that hunted deer regularly would have realised that they do not outlive humans. The "age of a deer" could just have been a metaphor for a bloody long time, or it may have referred to a specific number of years. The idea of animals (at least the magical ones) having inordinately long life spans is a common one. In the Welsh Triads, the oldest things in the world are three birds:

Three Elders of the World:
The Owl of Cwm Cowlwyd,
the Eagle of Gwernabwy,
and the Blackbird of Celli Gadarn.

The ancient tribes had laws not just to protect human life, but animals as well. Most of these laws related to domesticated animals. For example,

It is illegal to over-ride a horse, force a weakened ox to do excessive work, or threaten an animal with angry vehemence which breaks bones (i.e. beat it senseless).

Many birds, insects, mammals, reptiles, fish etc cropped up quite prominently in myths, too many to cover in any depth at this stage. Let us take a brief look at a few creatures that appear:

The wild pig was considered an emblem of ferocity and strength, suitable to warriors. A number of helmets have been dug up featuring pig motifs, and many of the trumpets blown in battle (called carnyxes) were shaped to look like wild pigs or wolves. The Gaulish god Moccus takes his name from the word for pig, whilst the Orkney Islands were named after the pig tribe. Stepping on a boar's bristle after breaking a *geas* against hunting boars killed Fionn. King Arthur fought boars that had bristles of gold or silver. When Menw tried to steal treasures from the King of the Boars, Trwyth, he was only able to take a bristle.

In the '*Tàin Bó Cúailnge*', the two great magical bulls were the last incarnation of rival Druids. They started life as Fruich and Rucht, two swineherds. Friuch, whose name means, "bristle", became the Brown Bull that finally triumphed at the end of the *Tàin* over Rucht, whose name means, "grunt". Swineherds often have magical powers, and it is widely thought that the term is used as a metaphor for druidic keepers of the sacred animals. The Celtic religion was unusual in the high status it accorded to pigs.

For the Jews, Muslims, Hindus, Sikhs and even some Pagan religions (such as the Egyptians) pigs were regarded as unclean. This probably had much to do with pork going off very quickly in hot countries where those religions originated.

Gwydion and Gilfaethwy were transformed into swine for a year and a day, and gave birth to a piglet that the wizard Math turned into a boy called Hwchddwn Hir. Culhwch was born in a pig run and raised in humble circumstances. A great white sow called Hen Wen ('the old white one') crops up in Welsh myth, and a sow (not specifically named) led Gwydion to find Lleu, when he was hiding in an oak tree in the shape of a wounded eagle.

The deer is a popular feature of many stories; Fionn Mac Cumhal was called Demne as a boy, meaning "Little Fawn". His son Oisín has a similar meaning to his name. The mother of Oisín, and great love of Fionn, was the deer-woman Sadb. A common motif in myth was the deer hunt, where the hunter would often become so engrossed that he would not notice that the deer had lead him through the gates of the Otherworld.

The popular Gaulish deity Cernunnos was depicted with stag antlers. There are quite a number of statues of antlered gods from all over the Celtic realms, though many do not have names so we cannot always be sure if they are representations of Cernunnos or some similar-looking deity.

One of the Gaelic words for a stag, *damh*, has given its name to the month of November, *Damhair*, when the red deer rutting season takes place. It is also a slang word for fucking!! The Irish goddess Flidhais is depicted as riding in a chariot drawn by deer. She too has a vast sexual appetite.

The Cailleach is described as a guardian of the deer herds over winter, and they are referred to as her cattle. Gwydion and his brother were turned into deer and, after a year being hunted in the wilds, gave birth to a fawn. Math turned the little creature into a boy called Hyddwn, whose adventures are sadly forgotten. Even St Patrick turned himself into a stag, by reciting a poetic spell that has become known as the Deer's Cry.

The horse was hugely popular, and formed the central focus in the cult that expanded around the goddess Epona ~ she became so popular that even the Roman army adopted her and spread her worship across the Empire. There was one Scottish tribe named after the horse, the Epidii, who lived around what is now Argyll.

A number of deities have horse-imagery in their names. The Uffington White Horse hill figure has been dated to about 3000 years old, and may well have been carved in honour of a deity such as Epona. A number of magical horses appear in myth, such as Aonbharr who belonged to Manannán and could ride as easily over water as land. The Dagda also has a horse called ocean, reinforcing the link between horses and water. The link is to both the sea and fresh water. There are a number of horse-spirits, such as the *Each-Uisce* ('water horse'), that lure foolish people into climbing on their backs, whereupon they gallop to the nearest river, jump in and drown the rider (whom they then eat).

Rhiannon was made to carry people on her back like a horse as a punishment for the presumed murder of her baby. A farmer drove off a creature that was trying to steal a foal on May Eve, and found the stolen child ~ presumably dropped by the beast in its flight. Another goddess for whom childbirth and horses are closely linked is Macha. To complete a stupid bet made by her husband, she was obliged to outrun the king's fastest horse whilst pregnant. She won the race, but collapsed and died giving birth to twins at the finishing line. Lugh was believed to have invented horse racing, and it became a major feature of Lughnasadh festivals, though horses themselves were first brought to Ireland by the joint efforts of Fionn and Manannan. Interestingly, the word jockey derives from the Gaelic word for a horse rider ~ *eochaid*. Eochaid is also one of the titles born both by the Dagda and by the king who first organised the Brehon laws, which has lead some to speculate they are one and the same (though the name is very common).

The swan features mainly in a romantic context. Swans are, indeed, one of the few genuinely monogamous creatures, and are the primary symbol of Óengus and Caer in their story where love conquers all. In one of the Irish tragedies the four children of Lir were turned into swans for 900 years by their jealous stepmother (who was childless). The swans retained the power of human speech, and the ability to make wonderful music. They generated such an aura of peace that people flocked from miles around to see them.

The salmon is commonly associated with wisdom. In Irish myth the salmon swims in a magical pool where nine hazel trees drop their nuts. It eats the nuts and so gains the wisdom of the trees. When Fionn mac Cumhall unintentionally tasted the salmon, he absorbed all the knowledge and magical insights. In some Welsh myths the salmon is listed as the oldest of all creatures. Prince Elffin found the child that grew to be called Taliesin, the wise magician, in a salmon weir. Gwrhyr (who could talk to animals) accompanied Culhwch as they met a series of magical animals. The oldest and wisest of all was the salmon of Llyn Llyw (the River Severn, where once stood a temple to Nodens bearing carvings of salmon.) Cú Chulainn used the hero's salmon leap to cross the dangerously narrow Pupil's Bridge at Scáthach's stronghold on the Isle of Skye.

As you can see, a number of animals were often seen as having a close association with certain tribes. This phenomenon is widespread, and can be seen in the tribal societies of Australia, America etc. Certain Scottish clans claim descent from selkies (seal-people), and it may once have been the case that many tribes felt themselves to have an animal ancestor. Similar stories can be found elsewhere, such as the Pawnee tribe in North America who regard themselves as descended from wolves. Such tribes often tend to view the animal as a close relative, and treat it with especial respect. Food-restrictions are not uncommon, reminiscent of the *geas* against Cú Chulainn eating dog flesh. Many such tribes feel that the spirits of the animal in question guide and help them. This is the origin of modern ideas about totemism. Modern books tend to treat totems almost like astrological signs, and are very much geared to the individual finding themselves (most modern Paganism is very self-obsessed). In older times one of the central powers of the totem spirit was to unite the individual with others who were guarded by the same beast.

A number of myths account for certain species having kings. Triath, already mentioned, is the Irish name for the "King of the Boars". Dobharchú is the bloodthirsty King of the Otters. In Scotland the myth of Cluas Mór, the King of the Cats, remained until recent times, but with a Christian slant in that the King was seen as a demon. It may have been the case that there were once legends about the kings or queens of every native species going. Whether these monarchs were viewed as gods, fairies, or some kind of totemic spirit we no longer know for sure. Though you could, of course, try asking them and coming to your own conclusions.

Some questions for you to think about:
- Are there any particular animals to which you feel an especial kinship ~ maybe ones that often crop up in dreams, or that keep appearing either in real life and/or artistic representations?
- What do you feel about the way animals are treated in the 21st century ~ as pets, on farms, in circuses, zoos, the wild etc?
- Have you attempted to work with animals in a magical/ritualistic context? This could be a pet or familiar in ritual, it could be divination by watching bird flight, invocation of an animal spirit etc.

Practical exercise:
Research a native animal that you are **not** familiar with. Find enough information to spend at least 10 minutes telling a friend

or relative about its life cycle, diet, breeding habits etc, plus any native myths or legends about it.

Can you see any parallels between the behaviour of this creature and human actions? If you wanted to honour this creature through ceremony, draw up the key points in its year ~ festivals to mark such things as mating and breeding seasons, or other important activities (such as shedding or re-growing horns, moulting, skin sloughing etc).

Chapter Fourteen

Herb Lore

Herbal remedies were popularly used throughout the ancient world. Whilst no truly old Celtic herbal books have survived, many medieval manuscripts are extant and give remedies that were probably quite similar to what the Iron Age peoples were using.

Irish myth gives us the story of the goddess Airmid, daughter of the surgeon deity Dian Cecht. Her brother Miach followed his father into the surgical arts (mastering the skills of organ transplant and reattaching severed limbs). Following a family row, Miach was killed and 365 herbs grew from his grave. Airmid gathered these herbs and laid them on a cloak, placing each one over the part of the body that it affected. Her father did not wish this knowledge to fall into mortal hands, and so scattered the herbs. Only Airmid can remember what each does. We can only speculate that the early healers may well have used 365 plants, and learnt the uses of each one. There is an obvious link here with the calendar, and the fact that there is one herb for each day of the year. In many cultures astrology has had a major impact on medicine for thousands of years, and it is possible that the Druids may, like so many other people round the world, have combined astrological and medicinal knowledge.

Another goddess strongly associated with the healing arts is Brigid. One of the three sisters who make up the Brigid is referred to as The Healer. The Gaelic word for a flame, *luis,* is close to the word for a healing herb, *lus* (and possibly the original form of the ogam letter L). The dandelion is one particular plant named after Brigid, in Gaelic.

Back in Chapter Eleven we discussed the role of hospitals and medical care in early Gaelic society. In addition to formally

161

trained healers, many people would have learnt some basic healing techniques passed down the generations ~ herbal concoctions for treating coughs, colds, bruises, sprains and everyday problems. Scottish women who conducted basic healing within the family were referred to as *Cailleach-nan-Cearc*, meaning old woman of the hens, and were much like the wise women of English villages. Many of the herbal cures and spells of the Gaelic wise women survived into recent times, and were recorded by folklorists. How old these traditions are is uncertain, but many do seem to echo the ideas of a much earlier period. Even the more recent ones are worth learning about, if they prove to work well (we shouldn't ignore something just because it is new).

A popular technique for healing was the *éolas*. This combined an herbal concoction with a prayer, chant or other spell that had to be sung over either the herbs as they were prepared, or the patient as they were healed. The Carmina Gadelica contains many such *éolas* spells, collected by Alexander Carmichael when he travelled the Scottish Highlands and Islands during Victorian times.

A good example of an *éolas* chant comes from the blind poet Ailein Dall. Another Victorian writer, William Sharp (using the pseudonym of Fiona Macleod), recorded Ailein's healing spell, which was used to cure an *amadán* (a madman or simple-minded person, the word can be used for either condition). The original version has one more verse invoking various Christian figures. The original last two lines of the section printed below called upon the Son of Peace (Jesus) and the Heart of Mary. We have changed them to make them usable in a Pagan ritual. The Yellow Shepherd and the Wandering Shepherdess referred to in the fifth verse are probably the sun and the moon respectively.

Deep peace I breathe into you,
O weariness, here:
O ache, here!

Deep peace, a soft white dove to you;
Deep peace, a quiet rain to you;
Deep peace, an ebbing wave to you!

Deep peace, red wind of the east from you;
Deep peace, grey wind of the west to you;
Deep peace, dark wind of the north from you;
Deep peace, blue wind of the south to you!

Deep peace, pure red of the flame to you;
Deep peace, pure white of the moon to you;
Deep peace, pure green of the grass to you;
Deep peace, pure brown of the earth to you;
Deep peace, pure grey of the dew to you,
Deep peace, pure blue of the sky to you!

Deep peace of the running wave to you,
Deep peace of the flowing air to you,
Deep peace of the quiet earth to you,
Deep peace of the sleeping stones to you!

Deep peace of the Yellow Shepherd to you,
Deep peace of the Wandering Shepherdess to you,
Deep peace of the Flock of Stars to you,
Deep peace of the Old Gods to you,
Deep peace of the Shining Ones to you.

Another popular magical healing practice was the *Beannachd na Cuairte*, which means "blessing of the circle". A large ring would be woven out of healing plants, such as woodbine, through which the patient could be passed (one person either side to support the patient's head and feet). Usually the person would be passed through three times, and then the decorative ring chopped up into nine pieces (or just burnt). The number nine crops up in various contexts in Celtic mythology, as well as appearing in Norse mythology where a disease-causing serpent was hacked into nine parts and nine healing herbs created from the venom. In Egyptian mythology an ancient papyrus describing how to defeat the serpent of chaos was divided into nine chapters ~ curioser and curioser!

Similar ideas can be found in other parts of the country, where a diseased person is passed through a man-made or naturally occurring ring. The Men-a-Tol stones in Cornwall have one big stone with natural hole in it, large enough to pass a sick child through for a blessing from the stone. Psychologists tend to get all Freudian and see images of vaginas and rebirth here, but we shouldn't automatically assume that our distant ancestors were as obsessed about such things as we have become since the days of Victorian repression. They may have recognised a power present in the stone, and have agreed on the passing through with the spirit of the stone, as a means of seeking its assistance.

The Welsh text known as the Red Book of Hergest contains information about herbal medicine, penned by Rhiwallon Feddyg, who founded a medical dynasty often referred to as the 'Physicians of Myddfai[30]'. The family were Christian, like most people at that time, and the book contains many references to Jesus, Mary and the Saints. The book contains a whole list of diseases and the herbal concoctions used to treat them. One of the botanical gardens in Wales today is trying to re-grow a lot of these herbs.

Sticking with the earlier theme of nine sacred things, we will have a brief look at nine herbs used in Britain for many centuries. Before getting over-excited and running out to use these (or any other) plants, bear in mind that first it's worth learning about safe doses, learning to tell the difference between healing herbs and poisonous ones etc! You might also want to give some thought to how you gather them ~ make sure not too pick too many, or the crop might not be there next year.

Talk to the herb before you pick it. Plants have spirits too, and can be communicated with. The plant may be willing to give a few leafs, flowers etc in exchange for an offering. If it can be taken willingly, the potency of the plant is quite likely to be improved.

Críos Cú Chulainn ~ Meadowsweet (*filipendula ulmaria*). This beautiful plant, whose name means Cú Chulainn's belt, has delicate white flowers that open in September. It derives its English name from its popular use in sweetening mead, and can still be used in this way when brewing mead for ritual usage. As the Gaelic name suggests, it was popularly associated with the warrior Cú Chulainn, there being a legend that he used a bath of this herb to heal himself when fevered. In the days before carpets, it was a popular herb for spreading on the floor. As people walked over it, the crushed leafs released a pleasant aroma. It was often recommended as a potion for treating upset stomachs.

Liath-lus ~ Mugwort (*artemisia vulgaris*). In Gaelic this means "the grey herb". Mugwort is popular still as a tea to aid clairvoyant skills and lucid dreaming. Stronger doses were also used for treating intestinal worms, constipation and menstrual cramps. In medieval times mugwort was used as a good luck charm for travellers.

Lus-na-fala ~ Yarrow (*achillia millfolia*). Before the introduction of hops, yarrow was a popular plant for making strong beer. Medicinally, it was very popular for treating fevers and for assisting with liver illnesses, and the name has the appropriate meaning of 'herb of the blood'. It was also commonly used to treat cystitis, and used externally for cleansing wounds.

Suibheag ~ Raspberry (*rubus idaeus*). As well as the fruit being used for food and drink, the leafs can be made into a tea. This was often used to treat labour pains, but is best not given to women earlier on in their pregnancy. Stronger doses were often recommended to people suffering from diarrhoea.

Athair an Talmhainn ~ Camomile (*anthemis nobilis*). The flower heads and leafs remain popular as a tea for calming nerves and treating insomnia. It has also been used for curing diarrhoea, and soothing upset stomachs. Generally the tea has long been used for curing indigestion. The name means, 'father of the earth'.

Bainne Bó Buidhe ~ Cowslip (*primula veris*). The Gaelic name means 'milk of a yellow cow'. Cowslip wine used to be a very popular tonic. A balm can be made from the flowers, which are best collected in spring, which helps with sunburn, and some other skin problems. Herbalists treating arthritis often use the flowers. The root helps with conditions like whooping cough and bronchitis.

Bearnán Brighde ~ Dandelion (*taraxacum officinalis*). As the Gaelic name suggests, this plant is especially associated with Brigid (both the saint and the goddess). Its main use was a diuretic, helping people piss more - which cleanses the system of toxins. It was also frequently used in the treatment of jaundice, and a few other liver conditions. Dandelion leafs can also be added to salads.

Some questions for you to think about:
- Have you used herbs before to any extent ~ in cooking, brewing, healing, spells, incense making etc?
- Have you ever attempted to communicate with a plant, or felt any sort of sapient presence from one?
- Have you ever gone vegetarian, or changed your diet in anyway to include foods that you thought might be healthier? How did you feel?

Practical exercise:
If you haven't already got one, create an herb garden (use a trough if you live in a flat). If you already possess such a thing, use edible herbs to create a healing concoction for yourself, a pet, or another person. Check that none of the herbs would be adverse to the person being treated first!

Chapter Fifteen

Sacred Trees

Popular imagination intimately links Druids with trees, and for once this perception is a valid one. In the next lesson we will look at the Ogam alphabet, which has strong tree symbolism, and continue with our exploration of trees in myth and magic. For this lesson we will have a more general look at the role of trees in Celtic culture and religion, to set the scene for Lesson Sixteen.

If we go back far enough in time, early Britain was covered with forests. Back then trees must have seemed as plentiful as blades of grass are now. The sort of concrete jungle we have transformed our world into must have been unimaginable to our early ancestors, who could scarcely have thought of a world as soulless as ours. Though, sadly, this did not stop several tribes using slash-and-burn farming techniques, which deforested large areas and turned them into moorlands.

From a purely practical point of view, trees played (and continue to play) a vital role in human survival. The old tribes built their houses from wood, depending on trees for firewood, the materials with which to build boats, make tools, carve religious statuary, harvest fruit for themselves and food for their animals. It can scarcely be any wonder that those people viewed trees as holy things.

Such was the importance of trees, that the Brehons introduced laws to protect them. In one of the earliest examples of ecological law making, the Fenechus introduced penalties for people who felled trees without permission. The following excerpt is a poem from the *Crith Gablach*:

Cia annsom fidbeime   What are the most oppressive cases of tree-cutting

fiachaib baeth?	for which fools are fined?
Briugid caille,	The hospitallers of the forest,
coll eidnech.	the ivied hazel.
Esnill bes dithernam	A danger from which there is no escape
dire fidnemid nair.	is the penalty for felling the sacred tree.
Ni bie fidnemid	You shall not cut a sacred tree and
fiachaib secht n-airech,	escape with fines for the seven noble trees
ara teora bu	on account of the fine of three cows
inna bunbeim bis.	that is fixed for cutting its stem.
Bit alaili secht	There are others, seven
setlaib losae.	atoned for in seoit [money] due for undergrowth.
Laumur ar dochondaib	Let me venture for the benefit of the immature
dildi cailli:	to state the immune things of the forest:
cairi fulocht benar,	a single cauldron's cooking wood that is cut,
bas chnoe foisce	a handful of ripe nuts
frisna laim i saith soi.	to which one stretches not his hand in satiety.
Slanem de	Freest of all
dithgus dithli.	is the right of removal.
Dire ndaro,	The penalty for the oak,
dire a gabal mar,	the penalty for lobbing its larger limbs,
mess beóbethad;	with its life-sustaining mast;
bunbem n-ibair	the trunk-cutting of the yew;
inonn cumbe cuilinn,	the same penalty for cutting the holly tree.
Annsom de	Most oppressive of all
dire secht n-aithlech	is the penalty of the seven commoners of the forest
asa mbi bó:	for each of which there is a cow of payment:
bunbeim beithe,	the trunk-cutting of the birch,

baegal fernae,	the peril of the alder,
fube sailech;	the undermining of the willow,
dluind airriu aithgein	declare restitution for them,
anog sciath	the maiming of the hawthorn
sceó draigin;	and of the blackthorn;
dringid co fedo forball,	its restitution extends to the undergrowth of the wood,
forball ratho,	the undergrowth of fern,
raited, aine,	of bog-myrtle, of reeds,
acht a ndilse do flaithib.	save that these are free to lords.

As you can see, a whole list of fines applied to anyone who wantonly hacked down trees or even lopped off branches without gaining consent from the local lord. In addition to the *Crith Gablach*, there is mention of a law book called the *Fid-bretha*, the Law of Trees, however this text has been lost to time. *Fidnemed* is one of the words for a sacred grove of trees ~ one probably used for ritual. The word for an individual sacred tree is *bile*, and there are various places in Ireland that take their name from a holy tree that once stood there.

This list, which is backed by other sources, divided trees into three categories according to the size of the fine payable for each ~ oak, hazel, holly, yew, ash, pine and apple are classed as *airig fedo*, "nobles of the wood". One text states that this is because oak has acorns and nobility, hazel has nuts, apple its fruit and bark, yew because it is good for building, holly for making chariot-axles, and ash for spear shafts.

Alder, willow, hawthorn, rowan, birch, elm and cherry were counted as *aithig fedo*, "commoners of the wood". Blackthorn, elder, spindle tree, aspen, juniper, whitebeam and a now rare tree called arbutus were called *fodla fedo*, "lesser divisions of the wood". The lowest class, *losa fedo* or "bushes of the wood" included bracken, bog-myrtle, gorse, bramble, heather, briar and broom.

Various stories talk of tribes having trees that were regarded as especially sacred. In Ireland there were five famous trees, all planted by Fintan. As discussed in an earlier chapter, a giant (who was probably meant to be an angel) attended an assembly at Tara with a branch bearing nuts, apples and acorns all at the same time. He lived on the smell of this fruit while teaching the people, and gave some berries to Fintan. He then planted the seeds around Ireland, where they became magical trees of huge size ~ the Ash of Tortu (*Bile Tortan*), the Yew of Ross (*Eó Ruis*), the Yew of Mugna (*Eó Mugna*), Dathi's Ash Branch (*Craeb Daithi*) and the Ash of Uisnech (*Bile Uisneg*). Trees such as this were often tied to the happiness and success of the tribe in whose territory they grew. This myth describes trees being deliberately planted, so it may well be indicative that ~ despite being surrounded by dense forests ~ the old tribes might have planted saplings for special occasions or ritual use. Even if they didn't, it's something to be heavily encouraged these days, to help reverse the trend to concrete over everything in sight.

Trees were so important to some tribes, that they named themselves after them, such as the Euburones (the Yew People), and the Lemovices (the Elm People) of Gaul. Accounts of forest spirits are prominent; such as the moss covered *gillie-dhu* who guards the woods and occasionally helps lost travellers. The Russians have a similar story, about spirits called the Leshii, the Greeks have Dryads, and even Tolkien took the idea and came up with the Ents.

Many ancient (and modern) people regard trees as sentient, thinking creatures. A common notion is that they harness the myriad number of creatures that depend on them (birds, squirrels, rabbits in the roots etc) as eyes and ears to observe things over a greater range ~ so overcoming the fact that they cannot walk. Though there are many old stories of trees that do occasionally go for a wander! A birch lives about the same length of time as a human; an oak tree averages 900 years, whilst a yew can live for thousands of years. Think of the amount of wisdom and understanding a 2000 year old yew tree might have amassed! Some trees might actually remember the original Druids gathering near them. It's small wonder that trees are held as sacred in just about every religion going. Many faiths have the idea of a cosmic tree, or one particularly sacred tree. The Heathens have the idea of Yggdrasil the World Ash (or possibly Yew), Buddha found enlightenment meditating under the Bo Tree, Eden was home to the Tree of Knowledge of Good and Evil etc. The Irish god Bilé shares a name with the sacred tree, and many writers postulate (though others strongly disagree) that he is the Celtic version of a world tree.

Folk traditions advise people wanting to cut off branches, or chop down whole trees, to speak to them first. Certain species (such as the elder) are said to be particularly vindictive if they are cut without consent. Several traditions recommend leaving an offering ~ either a libation, or often a coin buried in the roots. If you do ever need to chop the whole tree, it would be a good idea to plant several more in recompense.

Botanists have come round to the idea that trees communicate with each other, mostly through the release of chemicals. In 1979 a chemist called Rhoades carried out an experiment with willow trees that suggested when one tree was under attack from bugs, it could send out a warning to other willow trees that would then produce chemicals to defend against the bugs. Jeanne McDermott, another researcher, published an article in 1984 backing this up with further studies of her own. Such research is still in its early stages, and there may be more ways for trees to communicate than just releasing pheromones. One day it may be possible for science to show how trees communicate with humans as well.

As the Ice Age began to recede in Europe, a variety of trees sprang up. In most of Europe the birch and hazel were amongst the first, followed by the Scots pine and juniper. Later on came the oak and alder. About 7, 500 years ago the land bridge with the continent was washed away. Those trees (and animals) here before that date are the main ones regarded as native. After that date, mankind introduced other tree species, usually deliberately. In those early days most of the land was covered in forests. By the time of the Domesday Book, only 20% of the land was wooded. The rate at which farms, towns, roads etc have swallowed up the woods has been alarmingly fast. Many charities have been set up to preserve surviving woods, or plant new ones, but it's never likely to be more than a cosmetic move unless there is a drastic reduction in the size of the human population of these islands.

Some questions for you to think about:

- Have you a favourite species of tree? If so, what is it about that tree that you most like?
- Are the feelings you get when walking in a wood different from those when walking on the beach, in the mountains, through a town etc? Do you get different feelings in different types of forest ~ such as between deciduous and coniferous?
- Have you ever planted a tree to mark a specific event in life ~ a birth, marriage, death etc? Did you plant whatever tree was available, or choose a particular species because it suited the occasion?

Practical exercise:

Find a tree and talk to it! Spend time quietly meditating... make offers... compose poems in honour of it... sit and listen to what it says, what images come into your mind. In the longer term, try going back to the tree in different seasons and keep a diary of how its moods change. Try to talk to other trees of different species, to see if you can pick up on distinct qualities.

Chapter Sixteen

The Ogam Alphabet

The Ogam is an ancient Irish alphabet. It consists of twenty symbols or letters called *fid* (singular)/*feda* (plural). See Appendix 3 for an example. In a later version an additional five were added, called the *forfeda*, to enable the spelling of dipthongs. These symbols were mainly intended to be written in vertical columns, usually starting from the bottom and writing upwards. They lack the aesthetic beauty of runes or hieroglyphs, being simply horizontal and diagonal lines cutting across a central stem (called a *druim*, or ridge). The twenty symbols are divided into four sets called *aicme* (meaning 'tribe') with five symbols in each set. The oldest ogam symbols date from some 1,600 years back, appearing on stones in Ireland, Scotland and those parts of Wales and Cornwall colonised by the Irish. Nearly all of these examples are grave markers ("Ammecatus son of Rocatus lies here") and many may have served as boundary markers too.

The monastic authors of the histories believed that ogam existed long before the period in which they were writing - legends refer to the Druids using them carved on wood. Whether they were accurate in this belief is another question. One account describes them being the invention of Ogma, a member of the *Tuatha Dé*. No wood carved ogams have yet been found, though given the damp climates involved this is not surprising.

Some contention arises as the exact nature and purpose of the ogam. Some writers cite them as a Christian invention; mostly due to the fact that the stone carvings date from the early Christian period and are not used in an overtly Pagan manner (e.g. there are no surviving invocations to Pagan deities written in ogam, though equally there are no dedications to saints or other Christian figures). This claim does not address one simple question ~ why would they have bothered? Missionaries favoured the use of Latin as the language of the Church. Why go to the trouble of inventing a whole new alphabet, and such a clumsy one at that, when they could have used an existing alphabet such as Latin or Greek? It is not as if the stone examples convey any secret or mysterious messages between monks. They are quite prosaic in nature. We know that the Druids survived for several centuries alongside the Church, so even to refer to the 5th to 8th centuries in Ireland as "the Christian Period" is misleading ~ it was a mixed faith period. Why then place the ogam only in the hands of the Church ~ or, for that matter, only in the hands of Druids? It may well have been used by both faiths at different points.

At this point it is worth returning to a point made earlier in the book about the differing purposes of historical artefacts. For many professional academics the ogam alphabet is a thing to be studied in its historical context ~ what it meant to the people who originated it; why they developed it; what they used it for etc. Such issues do hold the attention of some modern Pagans too, however, on the whole most Pagans look at systems such as the ogam alphabet and wonder what they can do with it now.

The contention that the alphabet was a secret one also seems dubious. Grave stones and boundary markers, by their nature, are public signs intended to be read by the literate. Why write a public message in a language most people cannot read? It would be like putting British street signs in Chinese ~ pointless. Though it may have been done for aesthetic purposes, like the modern tendency to use Latin inscriptions on official buildings, despite the fact that most of the populace cannot understand that language. However, the ogam alphabet is not particularly artistic to look at. The ogam may have started out as a secret alphabet, but by the 5th century it was probably fairly commonly understood. The Irish were regarded as a highly educated and intellectual society during this period, so more people may have been literate than we suppose.

Sean O' Boyle suggests that it served as a means of musical notation for the harp, probably stemming from the pentatonic scale of Celtic music (ogam being arranged in sets of five letters). It is unlikely to have started as a notational system, though it could well have been adapted to that use at a later stage much as letters from our modern English alphabet are used in writing musical scores. However, the medieval texts make no mention of such a use. We are inclined to think that Shin Ogam (or something similar) was the earliest form. It started out as a sign language, with words communicated by placing the fingers either side of the shin, or a sword/staff/straight object of some description. When a written language was required scribes simply wrote symbols that were a direct copy of the hand gestures. The awkwardness of the written alphabet suggests to us that it was never intended for writing sentences of great length. It was, perhaps, either just for shorthand, or mostly for magical/symbolic use.

Of greater interest to most modern Pagans than basic alphabets or musical scores, is the use of ogam in magic. Each ogam is associated with a set of meanings described in the '*Auraicept na nEces*', the core of which dates back to the 700's. This tome mentions the existence of 150 variants for each letter ~ some of these are just differing written symbols for the same letter, some are forms of sign-language for non-verbal communication, and some are definitely of Christian origin, such as Saint Ogam. Mastering these 150 types was intrinsic to the *fili* progressing through the seven grades of accomplishment. Those variants that might most strongly inspire modern Pagans include animals, trees, weapons of war, colours etc. Though often referred to as 'the Tree Alphabet', trees are but one of the sets of meanings attributed to them.

There is some debate as to how the ogam originated. Did it start out as a system of hand signals, only later becoming a form of writing, or vice versa? Were some of the letters named after trees, or the other way round? From a pragmatic point of view the system can be used magically without ever needing to resolve such questions. Legends frequently refer to their use in the casting of spells, rather than viewing them exclusively as an alphabet. There are accounts of them being carved onto branches and then being hurled at people to release their magical effect.

Conflicts can arise between some Pagans and some academics as to the nature of the ogam. Partly this may stem from each side not quite understanding the agenda of the other. Historians and linguists tend to study the ogam within a chronological setting, asking questions in the past tense: what were the ogam letters for, how did the ancient Gaels understand them etc. Beyond wanting to publish books and articles about it, academics are not, as such, trying to *do* anything with the ogam alphabet in a present-day context. Pagans, conversely, tend to have a more limited interest in how people over a millennium ago viewed the alphabet. Their main interest is often in what uses those symbols can be put to in the here and now. Justification for those uses is often sought but seizing on any evidence (even if quite slight, or perhaps coming from a dubious source) that creates a sense that these modern applications are not just made up, but have some pedigree behind them. Going on purely anecdotal experience, it seems to me that very few Pagans engage in this emotionally invested quest for a contemporarily useful symbol set with any degree of venality. Whilst there are certainly a great many silly things said in the wackier end of the New Age market, most of it probably stems from naivety rather than a conscious desire to deceive.

A noticeable distinction within modern Pagan outlooks is between those who regard magical power as innate and those who see it as projected. The former tend to regard the world as having its own inherent spiritual presence, akin to the Japanese concept of *ki*. This school is inclined to view alphabets such as the runes and ogam letters as having their own innate mystical power, recognised by modern Pagans. The second approach assumes that many things have no actual power of their own, but are merely props that help the human mind shift into a suitably liminal state. For such an outlook, the ogam letters are just shapes on a page with no intrinsic meaning beyond that which any given person or cultural group (be they in the 5th century or the 21st) opts to invest in them.

For those who adhere to the latter notion, any group of modern Druids is free to use the ogam symbols (or any other group of sigils) for any ends they feel like and to impart any meanings they desire to them. Which does not give them liberty to claim that other groups (such as 5th century Irish scholars) shared their ideas or habits.

Amongst those of the former approach, there is more likely to be a desire to delve into the past and to try and maintain a harmony of usage and interpretation between the present and the distant past. If a sigil genuinely does have an innate quality, then it follows that whoever came across the letter first would have recognised it.[31]

Modern Pagans tend to want the ogam letters to be useful in magic, divination, and as a meditation aide. It could be argued that modern Druids suffer from rune envy[32], and are reading more into the ogam than the limited historical evidence can support. Or it may be considered that they are responding to the inherently magical nature of the alphabet, even if it is often in ways that would make no sense to people from CE 400.

It is probably also worth pondering on why people in the 21st century would want a magical alphabet, be that ogam signs, runes, hieroglyphs or anything else. Doubtless there is a partial appeal to childhood nostalgia for secret codes and wizards' tomes! However, there is more to it than just whimsy. As linguistic creatures we generate mental constructs of the world in words; language and the tools that construct it are potent tools in shaping of the world (and the potential to reshape it in ways more to our taste ~ the drive behind magic). We are not too far distant from the days of mass illiteracy, when the social power was intimately tied to the twin capacities to write and read. The creation of writing began the era of manuscript culture, when suddenly the intimacy of oral culture opened to the impersonal potentials of text. If I can record whatever ideas and knowledge are important to me, then I can transmit them over great distances to other people who can decode the squiggles on the page. Not only great distances, but great periods of time too. A scroll, like a Tardis, can travel over both time and space to encounter places that the author will never get to and people he will never live long enough to meet. Mass literacy in the West has made as rather blasé about the magical potency of writing, and we now have the infuriating prospect of both children and adults for whom reading is a boring chore they cannot be bothered to engage in.

Kemeticism, Judaism and Christianity are but three religions that view the word as miraculous, possessed of the power to create or destroy. If writing is so powerful, is it any surprise that assorted alphabets around the world are so laden with mythical symbolism?

In Chapter Four we touched upon the topic of the sacred land and how some parts of the British Isles are bejewelled with early stories that detail the spirit within local geography, whilst other parts of the land have lost whatever early tales were once told of them. Within Clan there is a goal to re-imbue our land with myths. It may be wonder if part of the interest in ogam and the much later Welsh *coelbran* stems from a patriotic kind of spirituality. Given that all mainstream religions originate from some other part of the world, it is not over-surprising that a fair few British and Irish people have yearned for native as well as (or instead of) imported spiritual practices. The same urge, perhaps, that lead 6th century monks to want to incorporate older Pagan stories into Christian accounts, rather than discard them entirely; or the urge that lead eccentric Victorians to want to link Ancient Britons with the wandering tribes of Israel. So now we have a quite understandable wish for there to be a sacred language which is tied to these lands in some way.

There is less limited indication of their use in divination, which seems to be their most popular function amongst modern Pagans. One incidence shows the identity of a headless corpse being established through use of ogam and other magical techniques. Such incidents tend to suggest that the ogam was not used for predicting the future so much as for elucidating the past and present. The modern way of divining with ogam is clearly heavily influenced by the use of the heathen runes. Twenty wooden lots are cut, each depicting one *fid*. These are then either drawn blind or are cast on to a cloth and the pattern divined. Although this seems a logical way to use them for divination, it cannot be said with any certainty that this was the way the ancient druids used them. These days the chronically lazy can buy sets of pre-chopped sticks with ogam burnt into them, or even have ogam cards ~ which are pretty, but seem to miss the point rather. The ogam staves referred to in myth are often on yew wood, a particularly hard wood to get hold of these days. A number of the *feda*, if inverted, look like other *feda*. To avoid this confusion the staves can be pointed at one end to tell which way is up. From a divination perspective, this also allows the possibility of reading inverted symbols. While there is no indication that the original Druids did this, it certainly allows for a greater degree of subtlety in the reading. Magical systems are organic, they must be allowed to live and grow rather than being artificially stunted into some Golden Age now long gone.

None of the surviving texts that mention ogam letters being used magically give detailed information on how exactly this was meant to be done. However, it is always possible that some previously unknown manuscript might one day be unearthed that will resolve this issue. Whilst we await further translations, the ogam can be understood from references in histories and (more importantly) from direct experiences with the Gods and with the energies in question. The letter (*Duir* ~ D) represents the oak tree. To understand this *fid* one need but sit under a few oak trees and open one's psyche to their influence. Of course the trees (or birds, herbs, colours etc) may not relate to each person in exactly the same way. So there must always be room for individual interpretation. There cannot be an "official" set of meanings ascribe to the symbols, only the result of personal experience; though we have tended to find that most people come to very similar conclusions at the end of the day.

There is no ogam equivalent of the Anglo-Saxon Rune Poem to guide the magical practitioner. The closest we get is the Word Ogams of Morann mac Main, Óengus mac Ind Óic and Cú Chulainn, which do offer some commentary, though it is often obscure and confusing. Many people have interpreted the Welsh *Cad Goddeu* (Battle of the Trees) poem as relating to the Irish ogam, though many academics consider this to be a mistake and some see the *Cad* as satirical rather than mystical. There are a number of ways of using the ogam for magic, attested to in legends. The commonest way is to carve them on some object, imparting the power of the symbol to that object. Another is the use of *forcain*, a technique in Irish magic whose literal meaning is to 'sing over'. Any word or verse can be sung, including the names of the *feda* to raise the energy linked to the sound and direct it, for good or ill, at a desired target. As the word implies, this is normally done with the target present rather than as a form of distance magic. This practice can be combined with O' Boyle's ideas around harp scales, to consider the tone that a particular word should be chanted in.

Taking the ogam to a deeper level, they are not just to be studied as individual symbols. Each of the *feda* comes in a set, and these sets are gathered for a reason ~ the interlinking meanings must be sought. The *Auraicept* contains a mandala called Fionn's Window (though the word 'window' would be better translated as 'smoke hole' ~ the chimney at the top of every roundhouse). This arranges the symbols on five concentric circles, reminiscent of the rings on a tree stump. Each of these rings links four *feda*, and again there is a reason underpinning this. So the ogam letters contain countless layers, taking one ever deeper into an understanding of the Iron Age mind set, and what it can teach us now.

In creating a set of ogam staves for divinatory use it is best to start with an invocation to Ogma (in my opinion one and the same as the Ogmios of the Iron Age Gaulish peoples, though some historians dispute this), creator of the alphabet, to ask for his consent and assistance. This secured, it is time to find the wood. Different modern Druids give varied advice on this matter ~ some will carve each stave from the appropriate tree or bush (though some of the woods are brittle and unsuited to such use). Others favour making the whole set from yew, oak or rowan. If you have no strong feelings, meditate and see what Ogmios advises. Next you could go to a forest where the type of wood you desire grows ~ forests are preferable to harvesting from roadside or city trees, which usually have a thick covering of exhaust fumes and other pollutants. Speak to the spirit of the forest; ask for its guidance in finding suitable branches. We favour fallen wood, rather than cutting live wood. Having fallen the branch is already offered up, and taking it will not damage the growth of the tree. None of the surviving myths tell how ogam sets should be made, so this advice is based on experience rather than legendary precedence. Having acquired a suitable branch, take it home and dry it out ~ if the branch is recently fallen it may need several months to season. When ready cut the branch into twenty sections about the length and thickness of your index finger. Bigger than this they will be awkward to handle. Strip the bark or leave it on as your artistic sensibilities dictate. Point one end of each stave, so you know which way is "up". Slice a strip from the other end to make a flat plain on which the ogam symbol can then be burned with a pyrography iron. Paint it on if you prefer. Having completed the whole set, dedicate them to Ogmios and whichever other deities seem appropriate. Then you are ready to start divining.

There is some dispute as to which trees represent certain letters, and you will find three or four alternate versions of the tree ogam. Our understanding is that the Druids of old were pragmatic people who would have sought inspiration amongst whichever trees grew in their locale that most embodied the qualities the *feda* represented. So a Druid in the Scottish Highlands would probably have used different trees from one in Munster. For now let us just use the trees that we find most suitable. The alphabet only has 20 letters; so many modern letters do not appear in it. If you wish to write words in modern English (such as your name) using the ogam, try using those *feda* that are phonetically most similar to the missing English letters.

Using these points as guides, it may easily be extrapolated how the ogam can be used in magic ~ burning birch leaves during a banishing ritual, chanting the *Iodho fid* at a funeral, carving the *Muin* symbol in a talisman to expose a secret etc. As well as being used for magic and divination, the ogam symbols may also have used in poetry and storytelling as a means of allusion and metaphor. If in a tale a character falls asleep under an apple tree, the implied meaning is decidedly different from if he sleeps under an oak tree. Like any symbol-system, the understanding and usage of ogam is a mixture of researching how its originators perceived it and fusing this with ones own projections and experiences. Without wishing to get too obscure, a number of cultures have the concept of certain sounds having transcendent power ~ whether that be Hindus chanting *aum*, Heathens using *galdr*, or Kemetics intoning *ren*. Personal experience may help guide the modern practitioner to decide if the ogam alphabet is merely a prosaic array of sigils onto which ideas have been projected, or if there is any innate metaphysical power to them.

Ogam divination is growing in popularity, and many general New Age books will give a few pages over to it these days. Most of these books seem to be written by people who (one assumes) have never actually tried using the ogam, or done more than just gawp at a tree. It is possible to use the ogam for divination without practising or even having more than a superficial interest in Iron Age Celtic religion. However, to do so is to lose an awful lot, for it takes the ogam out of their context. To study the staves in any great depth one really does need to have a great interest in Gaelic spirituality and, ideally, be a follower of those Gods. Their greatest use for a modern polytheist comes as a meditation aid for spiritual growth, rather than exclusively in divination.

Some questions for you to think about:

- Have you ever tried using an alphabet (ogam, runes, hiero-glyphs etc) for magical or ritual purposes?
- Have you ever created your own (or purchased, or been given a) divination set? Do you divine much for yourself, or for other people?
- Have you ever thought about how magic works? Is it simply a matter of getting into the right frame of mind, or do such things as ogam-chants have a power all of their own? How might reciting a spell actually affect someone?

Practical exercise:

Create a set of ogam staves, if you do not already possess such a thing. If you do own one already, find a suitable time and place to sit and chant the names of the ogam. Try chanting in different tones to see which "feels right". Keep a record of any sudden insights, visions or experiences gained whilst chanting.

Chapter Seventeen

Druidry and Magic

Celtic legends are full of accounts of magic and spell-casting ~ magical mists that blind enemies, rains of fire, curses that maim and injure, healing wells, cauldrons that resurrect the dead, people who transform themselves or others into animals etc.

In this chapter we will aim to look at some of the attitudes towards, and philosophies behind the very concept of magic. First of all, what do we mean by magic? There is no clear-cut answer to this, but generally it can be taken as the ability to cause change in the world by means that currently defy scientific explanation. The means by which the change is instigated usually has no obvious causal link to the change ~ there is no reason yet offered by science (or by many practitioners of magic themselves) as to why chanting particular words should cure a disease, or why wearing an engraved piece of wood should enable the wearer to pass unnoticed.

There are innumerable books that convey the impression that wealth, romance and vibrant health can be had in exchange for prancing about a purple candle at the full moon. Clearly if it were that easy the world would be a far happier place than it currently is. Magic is not easy, and it cannot be learnt in five simple steps for a mere £4.99! Whilst magic can be used to heal or to aid with personal problems, it is perhaps best conceived of as a method of spiritual transformation. The rains of fire and resurrected corpses are best left in the realm of Hogwarts.

Different cultures have varying stances on the nature and purpose of magic, none of which are mutually exclusive. The Ancient Egyptians held to the doctrine of *Heka*, the notion that the universe is created (as an ongoing process) by the power of the spoken word. In this belief all things have their *ren*, or True Name (which is distinct from the mundane name used in daily life). To correctly pronounce the True Name of a person or thing was to create, or perhaps more appropriately recreate, it; to influence, shape and transform it. In this philosophy, the magician takes the role of Creator, becomes like Amoun-Re singing the universe into existence. It may well be that the original Druids also held to a similar idea, but if they did it has not survived the passage of time in written form.

What does come across as a dominant theme in Celtic mythology is the importance attached to shape-shifting, often called *fith-fáth*. Whilst the Egyptian magician spoke the universe, the Celtic became it. Whilst from a storyteller's view the tales of shape-shifting may be seen as a literary device to inject fun and adventure, from a mystics view they are a means of self-transcendence. In becoming a hawk, deer etc, the magician experiences life from a profoundly different viewpoint. Faced with a challenge the Druid becomes the thing most suited to deal with it. Whilst the stories treat the changes as physical ones, the modern reader is more likely to comprehend them as psychological change ~ entering a trance state and taking on the identity and mental patterns of another living creature. Clearly such a thing requires a massive amount of mental discipline and practice, and cannot be learnt from some codswallop book or by forking out a small fortune to go on a dire course run by someone with an increasingly healthy bank account.

Falling in love, seeing a spectacular waterfall etc are often described as magical experiences ~ meaning there is something wonderful, awe-inspiring and numinous about them. The accomplished worker of ritual magic will know that a ritual also needs to have that aura of profound excitement (or trembling dread, depending on the nature of the magic) about it for it to work. A bland, prosaic ritual will produce no effect worthy of mention. One can but wonder how many people these days find their lives to be magical, wondrous, and mysterious. In 2006 over 31 million prescriptions were written for various anti-depressants and mood enhancing drugs, costing the NHS approximately 411.1 million pounds. Clearly a large number of people find life desperately bland and unhappy. Ritual magic is far more to do with awakening to the glory of life than it is to do with the Hollywood nonsense of lightning bolts flashing out of wands.

Some religions direct their attention to an ethereal heavenly realm, scorning this one as a distraction. What we have sought to convey in this book is a spirituality very much rooted in the material world, one that finds awe and joy on Earth. We are not interested in turning people into frogs, but shape-shifting depressed people into exuberant and life-embracing ones.

It may be speculated that the runaway success of the Harry Potter novels and films (and many similar works) is partly geared by a deep-seated wish to re-enchant the world. Delightfully entertaining as such things may be, fiction ultimately cannot replace what is missing from reality (though it may inspires methods for doing so). To restore a sense of wonder, mystery and vibrancy to the world is no mean feat though, we suggest, a vital one. It is one of the key draws of mystical religions such as the one we espouse. Rationalists often bemoan the hold that "mumbo-jumbo" has over the modern world, perhaps missing the point that people crave something more than the prosaic world seems to offer. That they so often get taken advantage of by the unscrupulous is a tragedy.

Magic at its root is, or can be, a way of healing the mind and soul by restoring a sense of the numinous. Though, of course, there is far more to spirituality than simple therapy!

Virtually all ancient cultures have accepted the idea that magic is real. There are varied accounts for how it happens, but many feature the idea of some sort of mysterious power or energy that mystics and magicians can tap into. Some cultures see this force as benevolent and positive, others as neutral and morally akin to electricity ~ in that electricity will still work regardless of whether it is being used to power a life-support machine or to torture someone to death. Unfortunately so much of early Celtic philosophy has been lost that we no longer have a complete or reliable picture as to exactly how the early Druids conceived of magical power.

In animist cultures much of what might be classed by outsiders as magic often involves the mystic communing and negotiating with the spirits that animate the world. Spells, if such they can be called, are often more meditative and similar techniques by which the sprites of tree, rock, river or animal may be spoken to and persuaded to the human agent's point of view. Within out practices in Clan, this is primarily what we do ~ talk to Gods, ancestors, and assorted animating spirits and negotiate with them. The kind of magic that you may have found described in assorted New Age books has no appeal to us.

Modern books on magic tend to emphasise ideas heavily influenced by the development of psychology since the work of Freud. Here magic is seen as primarily a matter of self-belief, where the intention of the magician is far more important than the ritual trappings of coloured candles, incense, talismans etc. If the magician believes it will work, then it will ~ regardless of what tools may be used. In this approach, all the candles, robes, herbs etc are basically theatrical window dressing to support what goes on in the magician's head.

Certainly practical experience shows that placebo is a strong factor in magic, particularly where a problem can largely be solved by putting someone at their ease or trying to achieve a change in mental state ~ spells to make people more confident etc.

A person who believes herself to be ugly and unattractive will behave in ways that discourage contact from others, which will then reinforce the notion that no one fancies her in the first place. If her self-image changes, then her behaviour is likely to change ~ she will act in a confident, outgoing manner that is likely to attract attention. She may start dressing differently, being more talkative, attending new places etc. Plus she is likely to notice when people are flirting with her, rather than wallowing in self-pity and dismissing friendliness as mere patronising kindness. For such a person, casting a "love spell" may be more a case of transforming her self-image than necessarily of conjuring cosmic forces.

Several ancient cultures believed that some things had their own innate power, independent of the magician. So there is a Germanic story of a man who accidentally caused a woman to fall ill by carving the wrong runes on a talisman ~ regardless of what he intended the talisman to do, the runes worked their own magic.

There is evidence that the insular tribes favoured this approach, regarding certain things (such as trees, rocks, ogam letters etc) as having a power all of their own, which the magician could not change or over-ride. The Druid exists in a world full of spirits ~ even if he does not call directly on a god to work a spell, he will be in a particular place whose *bocanach* may or may not support the spell; may wave a wand that has a sentient spirit; may stand near a bonfire that is alive and watching what goes on etc. All these spirits may choose to help, hinder, or ignore the spell being woven. It would be a foolish Druid who decided to work magic without bothering to first check if the spirits around him were in harmony with his aims.

Can a spell to cure a cancerous tumour be cured by placebo alone? If it could then, arguably, that power would be pretty damned magical in itself. However, most people would suggest that the ability to dispel a tumour requires more than just a bit of nebulous "positive thinking". It suggests the presence of a very real magical force that can make a measurable change in the body. Various cultures around the world have given this force a name ~ the Far Eastern countries speak of *chi* or *ki*, for example. It is uncertain what name the old Druids would have used for this power, assuming they even had such a concept in the first place. A popular term (since the publishing of Iolo Morgannwg's colourful book *Barddas* in 1862, which gave the word a new spin) is *nwyfre* ~ a Welsh word for firmament that some have taken to mean a magical force akin to *chi*. Linguistically, there is no metaphysical association with the word and the notion that it does have some numinous meaning seems to be a fairly recent one.

There is no suggestion from the old texts that other Welsh writers used the word *nwyfre* to mean anything other than "firmament", but that is the context that it is increasingly used these days.

In looking for metaphysical concepts, some modern writers prefer to use the Irish word *anam*, which simply means spirit or soul. Yet others (especially those in OBOD) use the Welsh term *awen*, or its Gaelic equivalent of *aí*, or sometimes *imbas* (which means spiritual enlightenment and, as such, is perhaps more the end goal than the means of getting there). All these words mean poetic inspiration, the sudden flash of the Muse that grants an artistic vision. In the medieval story of Taliesin, *awen* is actually a potion brewed up by Ceridwen. In the Irish tale of Fionn (with which there are decided resemblances) a similar power comes to the young hero when he accidentally imbibes the juices of the Salmon of Wisdom. Both have the idea of this transcendent force being a liquid, and in both stories it is accidentally consumed rather than going to the person for whom it was intended. This could suggest the use of some sort of concoction, perhaps a hallucinogenic. It might suggest an influence of the Christian notion of Divine Grace, which is visited upon people whether they appear to deserve it or not ~ or it may reflect an older idea that magical talent is transferred in some very curious way, unrelated to the amount of work an individual has put into study etc (a concept that may well appeal to the bone idle student).

Whatever term you wish to use is largely down to personal preference, given that we have (as yet) no concrete ideas as to what terms the early Druids themselves used. The underlying ideas tend to be rather similar ~ the concept that there is a power that moves through the universe, which can be harnessed by some people who know the arcane techniques and grants them amazing insights and understandings.

The Egyptians regarded *Heka* as an innate presence within the universe and believed a deity of the same name regulated it. It's quite possible that one of the Old Gods of the British tribes may once have been regarded as the origin or regulator of this dynamic power that enabled Druids to change into pigs, or turned gormless farm-boys into Chief Bards.

How a magical force, of whatever name, might work is difficult to say, given that we are only recently beginning to look at magic seriously again. Some of it may be argued as instigating changes in the mind, such as the previously mentioned love spell. Some may be direct changes at a physical level ~ such as the other case of banishing a tumour.

Like most old stories, the Celtic tales reflect magic being used to help or harm. In the latter case, magic is seen to affect people against their will. This clearly raises a raft of ethical issues for modern Druids that have been of less concern in the distant past. The stories suggest that people were largely unconcerned about violating freewill; if it was done to advance ones own tribe against enemy tribes. These days' people tend to be far less comfortable with such things, and generally speaking few of us are likely to be drawn into "battle magic" situations. Largely due to the twin influences of Christianity and commerce, we have mostly gone beyond tribalism and into a more universalist state of mind.

Most people these days would be uncomfortable working magic which tried to force another person to act against their will. It's also generally discouraged to use magic that causes outright harm towards another person (though there is plenty of evidence that the ancients thought nothing of asking the Gods to curse their enemies!).

Various styles of magic were used, some of which remained in use down into the Dark Age and medieval periods when the myths were being written down. One popular sort seems to have been chanted magic, and magic in the form of poetic verse. The spoken word was clearly regarded as having a great deal of power. There are accounts of Druids chanting over people whilst they went into trances.

More dramatic forms of magic involved calling up banks of fog to blind enemies, or flying through the skies. Whether anyone ever actually tried to do this, or it was simply the stuff of story-tellers, we don't know. Visiting ravening thirsts on enemies, or preventing them from pissing, also seem to have been quite popular ways of temporarily disabling people!

The accounts of magical healing have been discussed in previous chapters, but stories range from herbal cures through to the implanting of animal organs and even the re-attachment of severed limbs through chants and spells.

Shape-shifting has already been mentioned, and its importance cannot be emphasised enough. It forms the core of our approach to mysticism ~ transforming ones consciousness into something else, even if only for a short period, in order to learn something that will have a far greater effect later on. The goal of mysticism in some religions is to leave the physical world and its "distractions" behind, often with the implicit notion that the flesh is somehow corrupt and best eschewed. Such an approach sits ill with the passionate, life-embracing peoples described in Chapter One. Far from rejecting the world, *fith-fáth* seeks to embrace it in all its diversity, seeks to become bird or beast or tree. To echo the senti-ments of the early British (or some say Irish) heretical Christian monk Pelagius, if the Divine has formed the world then the world must be a good place. Those polytheists who feel the Gods are by-products of creation, rather than the instigators of it, can also echo this hedonistic vision.

In a related manner, to return to the story of the salmon, some forms of magic (such as the *tarb-feis* ritual in which a sacrificed bull was eaten by a Druid who would then commune with its spirit) involve eating a source of magical power. The Druid aims to make the source part of her, either by shape-shifting into it, or by eating it. Some forms of spell involve dissolving barriers in order to unite with a magical force, let it become part of you whilst you (in turn) become part of it.

A useful image to bear in mind is that of a spider's web, called a *cathan-aodaich* in Scots Gaelic, which is also a poetic allusion to the weaver's loom. The web is woven by the spider, which sits and waits for flies to land on the web. It senses the vibrations and acts accordingly. Our every action creates a strand of our personal web ~ each person we form a bond to, of love or hate, each place and object and idea we connect with builds up the network of the web... or weaves the cloth on the loom, for the arachnophobic! Everyone else is doing the same, so ultimately everything in the universe connects in some way or other to all the other webs. Clairvoyance can be thought of as rather like sensing a fly on the web, picking up on the emotions of someone to whom you are connected. Even the Gods are part of this, and weave their own exceedingly large webs as they go along.

Casting spells can be imagined as the deliberate attempt to weave our webs in a specific way ~ which is one of the reasons why so many spells require either the presence of the person to be affected, or some object linked with them. Where the link is weak, the spell will be ineffectual. The web, of course, is a two-way device: if you can sense and influence people to whom you are connected, then they can sense and influence you in return.

Some Pagan traditions have specific rules and ethical guidelines surrounding the use of magic. For us, we regard the ethics of taking magical action to be no different from the ethics of taking more prosaic actions. A person who regularly uses abusive magic is much the same as a person who hurts other people by physical violence. Such people invariably live in a state of fear that the people they victimise will one day seek revenge. Tyranny and paranoia frequently go hand-in-glove. Every action (or deliberate inaction) has a consequence for good or ill, the working of magic no different from any other area of life.

Of course, being a Druid doesn't make it compulsory that you have to cast three spells a fortnight. However, even if you have no interest in ever working magic yourself, it's a good idea to understand how it works and the ways other people might use it.

Some questions for you to think about:
- If a person doesn't know a spell has been cast on them, will it still work? If they know, but think it's all a load of rubbish, will that make them immune?
- Is there a situation in which it might be acceptable to use magic to force someone to act against his or her own wishes? What are the ethics of binding spells?
- Do some creatures, plants, objects etc have their own innate magical force? What happens if a magician tries to use some object in a spell that goes against the nature of the object?

Practical exercise:
Find somewhere quiet to meditate. Visualise a huge snake with the horns of a ram curling from its brow. The snake is coiled-up asleep but, as you watch, will begin to stir and lift its head. The eyes open, the tongue flickers. Try to be conscious of how you feel as the creature moves and shifts. It is of no threat to you and, having awoken for a few minutes, will then return to sleep.

Whilst engaging in this exercise, you may feel the urge to chant, sing, clap a beat with your hands, or do various other activities. Go with the flow, and see how the sensation of this creature awakening takes you.

Chapter Eighteen

Truth and Justice

In this chapter we will look at the unusual law codes of ancient Ireland, which are very similar to those of pre-Norman Wales (and so probably of the rest of Britain, once upon a time). In other chapters we have looked in more detail, now we will focus on how the laws illustrate the underlying principles as to what the old tribes considered justice to be. Having thought about human justice, we will have a brief reflection on the nature of divine justice and how the spiritual world works in this respect.

Most modern justice systems around the world tend to be based mainly upon the idea of retribution ~ legislators believe (probably correctly) that the public wish to see miscreants punished. Some countries favour imprisonment; others opt for flogging, chopping off hands, or other physical torments. The main emphasis in the Fenechus law system was upon restitution ~ the wish to see the victim compensated by the offender. This may be one of the reasons why the early insular tribes do not appear to have had prisons, and why the Fenechus laws made little use of execution, whipping or other such punishments. The rehabilitation of the criminal, or the deterrence of future crime, took secondary places to the healing of the wounds suffered by the victim and their family or protectors.

Not all societies think of crime in the same sort of way. The Laws of the Fenechus spoke of five primary categories of crime, defined in the 'Book of Aicill' as:

Five-fold are crimes:
the crime of the hand, by wounding or stealing;
the crime of the foot, by kicking or moving to do evil deeds;
the crime of the tongue, by satire, slander or false witness;

the crime of the mouth, by eating stolen things;
the crime of the eye, by watching while an evil deed is taking place.

Whilst modern Britain has the idea of slander and libel (crimes of the tongue), these are considered civil offences and are very difficult to deal with unless the person slandered is wealthy enough to afford fancy lawyers. The tribes took the idea of a damaged reputation far more seriously. Crimes of the eye is an unusual concept for us, in that it made *forcsiu* a criminal act ~ overlooking, or standing idly by and failing to report or intervene in an offence. We do have the idea of abetting after the offence (concealing someone else's crime), but *forcsiu* is rather more far ranging. This emphasises an important aspect of the Celtic approach to justice ~ law was held in the hands of all, not just a ruling elite.

Even whilst Ireland was becoming increasingly Christian, its laws retained the ideal of localised justice. This means that it was considered the responsibility of all citizens of the tribe to ensure justice was done, rather than simply to expect some external power (like the government) to come along and do it for them. Two good examples of this are the *digal* and the *troscad*, which were enshrined in law.

The *digal* was a form of legalised feud. If someone had been attacked in some way, and the criminal either escaped the courts or refused to pay what they ordered, then the wounded party could call a *digal*. This meant that any family, *ceilidh* (clients), bondsmen etc associated with the wounded party were obliged to hunt the criminal down and bring them to justice. Failure to take part in a legally sanctioned *digal* was itself a crime.

The *troscad* was a form of protest, commonly used in prisons around the world these days under the name of a hunger strike. Again, a wounded person in protest against a criminal who refused to pay their court fines could use it. The Brehon laws specified certain class boundaries as to who could use the *troscad* to protest against whom. The essential feature was that the aggrieved person should sit near the home of the person who had offended them, and starve him or herself. Every passer-by would be informed as to why the *troscad* was taking place, thus damaging the reputation ~ and so the honour-price ~ of the crook. Eventually most people would pay up rather than have their good names totally ruined by seeing the protestor die of starvation. It was not unknown for tradesmen with unpaid bills to use the same method to get justice (and payment). Should the person actually die, the target of the protest would have to pay damages to the family for murder.

The emphasis in these two examples is that justice is the responsibility of all people, not just something in the hands of kings and politicians. Translating this to an everyday level, if you are victimised by someone who appears to be eluding the courts, you have a responsibility to bring them to some form of justice. Likewise, one should support kith and kin when they have been ill used by some third party.

The ancient British and Irish appear to have had no form of police force to enforce laws, though they had people such as the *dalaigh* (barristers) to investigate crimes and present evidence of guilt or innocence to the judges and chieftains. If someone utterly refused to pay their fines or submit to whatever punishment was meted out to them, then there appears to have been little that the law system could have done to make them obey (unlike many countries where a militia could have been sent in to drag people to prison, or execute them). An interesting quote comes from Vincent Salafia:

> *The only executive authority in ancient Ireland, which lay behind the decision of the judge, was the traditional obedience and the good sense of the people. The public appears to have seen to it that the decision of the Brehon was carried out. This seems to have been indeed the very essence of democratic government with no executive*

*authority behind it but the will of the people, and it appears to have
trained a law-abiding and intelligent public.*

It may be worth pausing a while to consider how this contrasts to
modern attitudes to the law ~ have we grown too large as a society
to enforce the law without it descending into violent mob rule?
Can such a system only exist in a sparsely populated land? Does
it require everyone to have the same cultural values, or could it
operate in a multicultural country?

The many laws of Ireland (and maybe the same was true with
the British tribes before the coming of Rome) were revised every
three years during Samhain at the *Feis Tamhair* ~ the Great Feast of
Tara. This was a gathering of the brehons, chieftains and other
bigwigs. The brehons would recite the laws that existed, and then
the company would debate adding new laws, dropping out-dated
laws, amending inadequate laws etc. Doubtless all this pomp and
ceremony would have been attended with religious rituals,
feasting and celebration. In running a modern Druid group it
might be worth thinking about imitating this ~ perhaps having a
ritual once every three years where the "laws" and precepts of the
group are recited and revised.

Truth was an important concept to the old tribes. We have the
myth of the Cup of Wonder presented to King Cormac by
Manannán, after some grand adventures. If a person holding the
Cup ever spoke a lie, it would crack into three pieces (presumably
spilling mead all over them in the process). To mend the Cup,
three truths had to spoken over it. A not dissimilar legend was
told of a famous brehon who wore a neck torque that would
tighten every time he gave a false judgement in court, and then
loosen when he gave a true judgement. One of the Gaelic words
for deception or falsehood is *eitged*, which is mentioned exten-
sively in the 'Book of Aicill'. Poetically, it talks about white *eitged*
(smarmy flattery) and black *eitged* (satirical cursing), and allots
different levels of fine for different types of *eitged*.

Many religions have the idea of Divine Justice, which brings about both punishment of the wicked and reward of the worthy, even if human agencies often fail to do either. Hindus, for example, talk about karma ~ the idea that every action has a consequence, and that one must learn to live with (and learn from) the natural results of ones own deeds.

In Gaelic we have the word *dán*, which has many meanings. One of these meanings is fate, another gift or talent. Whilst, from an etymological viewpoint, these two meanings come from separate sources, they gel nicely. They convey the idea of fate, destiny, call it what you will, giving people gifts ~ almost like the Fairy Godmothers in Sleeping Beauty dishing out blessings. These gifts may be socially desirable skills, they might be strange things that society fears or disapproves of, they may be experiences that come in life for good or ill ~ but they are gifts, opportunities that are there to be seized and made the most of. As with many other cultures, a gift begets a gift ~ if fate gives you an opportunity which you take, there is an obligation to give something back. The talented poet might use their skill to praise the Gods, or lift people's hearts with beautiful words. The gifted doctor uses their skills to help heal people, perhaps especially those who cannot always afford medicines.

Fate, or *dán*, may be seen as visiting opportunities and gifts on people. Even if they don't always feel like gifts at the time! Look to what life offers as a potential opportunity to develop something useful to both yourself and the tribe. People who have lead appallingly dishonest lives may be given the opportunity to put right what they have done wrong, though whether they see this as a "gift" or not, is another question.

The early Celts appear to have had no notion of Hell, or any other place of punishment for the naughty. It may be that the wicked were considered to be given second chances to put right their mistakes, rather than being tormented for doing them. In a culture of recompense, the victims of wrongdoings may have been given back (in the Otherworld, or in some future incarnation in this world) the things that were taken from them.

Some questions for you to think about:

- In the modern world what is more important when dealing with wrong-doing (be it serious crime, badly behaved children, or whatever)... making the wrong-doer suffer, recompensing the victim, rehabilitating the miscreant, scaring other people off from committing the same crime, or something else again?
- The *troscad* is an example of ancient people taking responsibility for making justice happen within their own communities. What methods are available to you for bringing some miscreant (whether they have broken the law, or just offended your moral sensibilities) to justice?
- Hinduism has the idea of karma, and Christianity the idea of Heaven and Hell. Do you feel that the Gods take any part in the administration of justice (punishing the wicked, rewarding the good etc)? If human justice fails, and the innocent are wrongly punished or the dishonourable get away with things, is there any other force that can put right what has gone wrong?

Practical exercise:

Take part in a campaign for justice. This could be something like working for Amnesty as a letter-writer, or it could be going on a protest march for some cause you believe in, or trying to put right some injustice that you have either suffered or caused. The amount of time you devote to this is entirely up to you.

If you have the opportunity, sit in the public gallery during a trial (doesn't matter what for) as a means of seeing how the justice system in your country works. In the same vein, consider becoming a prison visitor in order to learn about that aspect of justice.

Chapter Nineteen

Poetry and Storytelling

Celtic culture, like many old tribal cultures, was and remains alive with a wealth of stories, legends, anecdotes and tales. That each new generation should have learnt the tales was vitally important, as the stories contained their very sense of identity. A people without stories are a people without a history, without a sense of who they are or where they are going. The possession of eloquence was seen as a gift as important to a warrior (let alone a Druid) as swordsmanship or archery. The Fenechus tells us:

> *Speech is given to three: to the historian-poet for the narration and relating of tales, to the poet-seer for praise and satire, and to the Brehon for giving judgement.*

One of the drawbacks we face as modern Druids is that the recordings of our myths did not take place until quite late, and then was done by members of a hostile religion. The Greeks, Romans and Egyptians were lucky enough to be having most of their myths recorded by people who actually believed in them, before monotheists put the boot in.

That the monks recorded the Celtic myths at all is something of a miracle, and testifies to the importance than even Christian-converts continued to place upon the culture of their Pagan ancestors. However, this does not mean that they recorded those myths completely accurately. We know that many stories try to squeeze in Jesus and other biblical figures. As well as adding bits of their own, they may well have dropped stories (or bits of stories) they felt were too unacceptable. So the tales we now have of the Dagda, Morrighan, Brân and Olwen are not likely to be the exact same stories that would have been told of the Old Gods by

Iron Age tribes ~ they are Christian versions of those stories. In the case of the Welsh tales, they were written down a long time after the conversion, when memories were that much dimmer than those that recorded the Irish tales. It seems highly unlikely that the Welsh chroniclers had any notion that the stories they were recording had ever had a polytheist context, but most likely considered them to be historical accounts of ancient monarchs, warriors and so forth.

Does this make the surviving early Celtic histories worthless to modern Pagans? The answer must be no, because ~ changed though they may be ~ they still contain clues to how the Gods were seen in purely polytheist times. There is also nothing stopping someone in the 21st century communing with their gods to find out the kind of stories they want told about them. There are far more gods named in the ancient world than are mentioned in the myths of the Dark Ages and medieval period. So clearly many myths have been completely lost. These medieval myths tend to portray the gods in a very human manner, no doubt influenced by a similar approach amongst the Greeks and Romans. Often the characters we now assume to be gods are not presented as divine at all, but as royalty or wizards and heroes. Bearing in mind that account of Brannus mocking Greek statuary at Delphi, it is possible that Iron Age tales did not see them as quite so human, but might have thought of them in plant or animal guise (the way some American Indian stories do), or as bodiless spirits and powers.

At this point it might be worth stopping to think what myths are. For some, they are just quaint stories to pass the time with. For early people they were ways of conveying messages about tribal identity and history, ethical ways to live, why the world is the way it is, what the gods and spirits are like etc. Without any stories at all, it is difficult to convey these complex ideas. Modern Britain is a garbled mix of many cultures and factions, such that we have few stories to bind us all together and give us a sense of who we are as a society. Perhaps this is one of the reasons why so many people feel disaffected, confused and alienated. These days we tend to think of stories as silly fantasies, or even as outright lies. Yet one person's "silly story" is someone else's truth ~ the record of who they are, what's happened to them, where they are going in the future etc.

Myths often formed centrepieces to the rituals of ancient Mediterranean Pagan cultures, acted out by priests at festivals playing the roles of gods, monsters and ancestors, and there is no reason to suppose that the Celtic tribes did not do something similar to bring their myths to life. The Welsh had the *cyfar-wyddion*, professional storytellers who travelled around acting as both entertainment and also repositories of lore. The Highland Scots and Irish still have the *seanchai* (though very few of them, these days), who remember the old tales and keep them alive for the next generation.

As well as stories, poetry was a major feature of life in ancient Britain and Ireland. The seven grades of the *filid* have been discussed earlier in the book. Research gives the possible meanings of these titles, though some words no longer exist in modern Irish and the interpretation is a bit speculative. Each rank had a whole list of things that had to be learnt in order to qualify for the next grade, showing that qualification for the next level was a matter of knowledge and skill, not some nebulous idea of mystical power. The seven grades and accompanying learning are listed in the Appendix. Whilst the choice of a sevenfold format was done to emulate the Church structure, the knowledge required at the various levels may well date back to Pagan times, when some other structure was in place. The highest rank of *ollamh* was said to have carried a golden apple branch, the *anruth* a silver one and all the lower ranks carried bronze branches. There were a huge number of poems and stories to be learned by the highest grade, not to mention an understanding of magic and the law.

One of the lowest classes of poet was the professional satirist, someone who made a living by cursing people's enemies by making up rude poems about them. Such people were not outside the law, and could not satirise just anybody ~ the potential to use them out of spite, or as a form of blackmail, was quite high. As the law tells us:

The satirist who satirises a guiltless person will grow blisters on his own face. And then he will die.

Satire was considered a very dangerous tool in the wrong hands, and will be explored in more depth in the future. As well as ridiculing the corrupt, poetry was used to praise the noble, sing eulogies at funerals, record some myths, call upon gods at ritual, record historical events, and to provide general entertainment. Poetry was also used as a form of magic, requiring a great deal of mental focus and emotional force. For the earlier cultures, words were very powerful things.

Poetry itself was a highly evolved art form. By the medieval period the Welsh bards were required to know 24 different types of metre, and be able to compose in them on request. Some of these forms can be used easily, even when writing in English, whilst others do not adapt very well to the modern English language. The Irish poets had fewer metres, though they were no less interesting.

Attendants at Eisteddfods recorded the Welsh forms in the 15th century, which derived their sources from much older poetic styles. The original date of some of these forms remains a mystery. Some additional types also existed, which had fallen out of favour by the 15th century. These included:

Englyn Milwr (or Triban) ~ *the Warrior's Song*
Englyn o'r hen ganiad ~ *the Song of the Ancient Strain*
Englyn Garrhir ~ *the Song of the Long Thigh*

Englyn Cildwrn ~ *the Song of the Clenched Fist*

The *pencerdd*, or Chief Bard (equivalent to the Irish *ollamh*), was expected to know all these metres by heart. A few of the metrical forms are explained below so you can begin to get some idea of what is involved. You might even want to have a go at practising some of the simpler ones. There is no suggestion that these metrical forms date back to ancient Pagan times, they are the creations of a Christian culture. However, they have their own innate beauty and the practice of metrical poetry is an excellent way of improving mental focus. The Engyln Milwr is the most basic of the forms ~

The **Englyn Milwr...** A moral poem that consists of three rhyming lines, each of 7 syllables. The 1st and 2nd lines describe the topic, and the 3rd line gives the moral or spiritual message. Before aiming for the division of meaning, just try writing three line verses with 7 syllables in each line (each syllable is represented by the symbol #).

A
A
A

An example of this (rhyming syllables in bold print) is:

*Forgotten lies the old **god**,*
*Deep beneath the useless **sod**,*
*No grave this, but sleeping **pod**.*

The **Englyn Penfyr** involves 3 lines. The first line has 10 syllables; the next two lines have 7 syllables each with a rhyming pattern as follows:

A # # B

205

B # # A
A

An example of this is:

*The old hunter sought the **beast** in the **night**,*
*Though without **might**, hope near **ceased**,*
*Yet frail, his skill found the **feast**.*

The **Englyn Unodl Union** involves four lines. The first line has 10 syllables, the next 6 and the last two have 7 each, with a rhyming pattern as follows:

A # #
A
A
A

An example would go:

*Lleu the maiden's call does **heed**, in summer*
*Indolent days oft **lead***
*To sultry nights and honey **mead**,*
*Sun's gift Man's deep thirst does **feed**.*

If we take a brief look at an example of Irish poetry, we will see that it is cyclical. The last word (or line) of the whole poem repeats the very first word (or line) of the whole poem, giving a sense of coming full circle. This technique is known as a *dúnadh*. In some forms (such as the one below) the very last word is not repeated, but must rhyme with the very first word. Irish poetry also makes use of the *aicill*, which is a moveable internal rhyme carrying over from the end of one line to the middle of the next. The **Ae Freisilighe** is an Irish metre that became popular in the Dark

Ages. Like most Irish poetry each verse has four lines. There do not seem to be any guidelines as to the subject matter for an Ae Freisilighe, so presumably you could write one about anything. The rules for structure are:

- The 1st and 3rd lines must end on a 3-syllable word.
- The 2nd and 4th lines must end on a 2-syllable word.
- However, it is only the final syllable of each line that need rhyme, not the whole word.

(# # A)
(# B)
(# # A)
(# B)

A not very good example of this, which can be blamed on the author, is ~

<u>Cú Chulainn at the Ford</u>
On Scathach's isle befrien**ded**,
Our sky bright then, no storm**cloud**,
With Ferdiad, belo**ved**,
Under blanket, not death**shroud**.

Quickly you flew resent**ful**.
Did you think me so shal**low**?
Were Medb's wiles so success**ful**?
Friendship left too long fal**low**.

The Ford, bitter mem**ory**,
Where love and hate so mud**died**.
Lots cast, we faced war**ily**,
Truth lost, broken and bloo**died**.

207

Red stream and red vic**tory,**
Friendship for honour t**raded,**
A boast made so hollow**ly,**
Over times past we w**aded.**

Now only spear penet**rates,**
Sunders both hearts, left life**less,**
My name this deed denig**rates**
Laeg's praise falls on me, worth**less.**

You blushed once, so wonder**ful,**
Now blanched, bereft of pas**sion.**
Forgive your Hound, remorse**ful,**
Think well of me in Tech **Duinn.**

The poem below is an invocation written to honour the brewing deity Gobanos (Goibniu, in the medieval myths). It is in **Rannaigheacht Mór** metre. This style has four seven-syllable lines, each of which must end on a one-syllable word with the rhyme scheme below:

```
# # # # # # (A)
# # # # # # (B)
# # # # # # (A)
# # A # # # (B)
```

The scheme can be one of full rhyme or of simple consonance. The third line has an *aicill* in the fourth line, which itself must end with two alliterating words.

World Wanderer knows the **need**
Of the parched world-weary **soul,**
Waters the heart's arid **seed**
With sweetest **mead** from blest **bowl.**

Forge's fire heats cauldron **deep**,
Melds honey to stream's pure **blood**,
White-hot blades from his coal-**heap**
For mead **weep**, slake in fresh **flood**.

Bee-rich steam censes his **shrine**
As swords in the waters **sleep**.
Blacksmith, beersmith, makes both **fine**,
Fighters and thirsters **dine deep**.

Where weapons wound, good ale **heals**,
King's hall with bright laughter **rings**,
The Lord before whom Truth **kneels**,
His heart un**seals**, sweetly **sings**.

Let all toast the Brew of **Age**,
Secret kept by clurichauns,
That restores youth to the **sage**,
Goibniu's **wage** to our great **world**.

The notorious Welsh mystic and author of somewhat dubious
texts, Iolo Morgannwg, popularised the term *Awen* to mean
mystical, poetic inspiration. It originally appeared in the story of
Ceridwen and Taliesin, where it was a magic potion that gave the
drinker amazing powers. That the potion flies out of the cauldron
in three drops has lead to all sorts of ideas buy later commentators. Some have seen it as a symbol of the Christian Trinity,
others as embodying the three aspects of the Wiccan Goddess, or
referring the three worlds (land, sea and sky). We no longer know
quite how the bards of Medieval Wales saw the idea of *Awen*.
Even less do we know how earlier peoples viewed the concept of
poetic inspiration.

In Gaelic, the term is cognate to *Aí*, which was also personified
in one story as the son of Ollam (himself a personification of great

wisdom) and was said to speak profound truths from the moment of his birth. Many modern Druids tend to chant the word *Awen* (or *Aí*) in their rituals, and sometimes prior to writing poetry. The chant may be believed to help gain a vision for the poem, or more often to raise magical power in the way that Wiccans will try to raise a Cone of Power. Others may use it more like a meditative mantra, to tune in to the Spirit. We have no evidence that the Druids of old chanted any of these words specifically, but if it works for you, go for it! Certainly one of the powers gained by Taliesin after consuming *Awen* (and by Fionn after tasting the juices of the Salmon of Wisdom) was an amazing command of poetry and language in general.

The word *Imbas* is sometimes also given as meaning poetic inspiration, though E J Gwynn translated it as supernatural enlightenment. In one short story Cú Chulainn encountered a magical being called Senbecc who was sailing up the Boyne in a bronze boat in search of *imbas*. In Gwynn's transation, Senbecc attained this state by eating the nuts of the magical hazel trees. The Ulster warrior tried to capture the strange man, but he escaped by playing the sleep strain upon his harp.

The consumption of hazelnuts may be an allusion to something involving the ogam letter Coll (hazel), though quite what we can only take a wild guess at ~ perhaps something akin to a chanted mantra, or possibly it was believed that meditating beneath these particular trees had some wondrous effect.

Poetry, like stories, can be used to convey very complex ideas and images in a way that laborious explanations fail to do. Few people in modern Britain seem to see poetry as a worthwhile thing; fewer still seem to regard stories as anything other than a way of sending kids to sleep at night. To convey the importance of both these art forms to our ancient ancestors and to the modern form of their spiritual beliefs can be remarkably hard.

Some questions for to think about:

- What stories do you have within your own family ~ tales about relatives living or dead, major upheavals you may have lived through (wars, emigration etc)? How are these stories kept alive within the family, or does hardly anyone in your family know much about past generations?
- What do you regard the central and important stories of your culture to be? Are you more familiar with old Pagan myths than with the stories told by the wider culture in which you reside?
- If a god has no surviving myths or stories, how might you go about learning their nature? Are stories actually necessary?

Practical exercise:

Write a poem in one of the above metres. Alternatively, tell a story at a festival, pub moot or other gathering. If you are a nervous public speaker, write the story down and just read it out to a group of known and trusted friends.

If you are studying this with a group of friends, you could divide a story between you and take it in turns to recite sections of a myth or a story of your own invention.

Chapter Twenty

Sacred Space

As we come to the end of the first set of twenty lessons, we now look at a number of related matters. Firstly, what is a nemeton ~ a holy place, what makes it sacred? Secondly, what do we know of how ancient Druids conducted rituals, and how can we conduct them now in the 21st century? Thirdly, how do we relate to the Gods in all this?

A nemeton is a place in which ritual is conducted. Often taken to mean a forest glade, it can refer to any place that is open to the sky. There were some long wooden buildings erected by the Celts, believed now to be temples, which appear not to have had roofs. The walls may have been for privacy ~ though that suggests there may have been people who did not attend the rituals ~ or perhaps to keep livestock out.

What makes a place sacred is difficult to answer. These days a building is considered holy if the people building it intended it for ritual purposes ~ such as a church or mosque. Some churches are in buildings originally intended for prosaic uses, like converted warehouses. Here a bishop or other dignitary usually consecrates the place. This is not dissimilar to Wiccans creating a sacred Circle in a place that is not usually viewed as magical. We do not know what the old Druids did to make somewhere sacred, if they did anything at all. Can a ritual invest a place with magical energy that was not previously there? When a Circle is banished, or a church deconsecrated, the idea is that the priest (or a deity) can take the energy away again. How do you feel this is possible?

Many religions, including that practised by the old Druids, have recognised holiness as being naturally present in some special places such as forest glades, waterfalls, mountain peaks etc. Some places have a presence all their own, which requires no building to be plonked there by humans. To borrow the Roman term, they are numinous.

Since the 20th century people have talked of ley lines, and widely recognised the idea of an energy field radiated by the Earth itself. More specifically, we have the idea that the planet contains many forces and energies, that certain of these presences are stronger in some places than others. When we speak of naturally holy sites, perhaps what we really mean is that some places are very strong in a type of power that leaves us in awe. There is not just one sort of sacred place but many, each with its own qualities. Some places exhibit the power to heal minds or bodies (or both), others induce a sense of quiet contemplation, and others fill us with vigour and excitement, yet others grant peace to the broken-hearted. Part of being a Druid is to be sensitive to the Land, to recognise what sort of qualities that meadow, woods, cave or house radiates. Having sensed what it is, the next step is to work with it. Having sensed that a place is deeply peaceful, it would be utterly arrogant to decide to conduct a victory ritual for success in battle. The activities carried out in a place must be in harmony with it. To do otherwise is like trying to carve wood against the grain.

Little is known of how the ancient Druids conducted ritual. Folklorists have suggested that some features of Irish Catholic practice, which have no particular root within Biblical or Vatican doctrine, may well be leftovers from an earlier age. An example of this is ritual circumambulation (walking round and round some holy relic or site). In Catholic practice this is usually done in a sun-wise direction for a fixed number of times, usually whilst reciting a prayer or saying a rosary. This activity can be seen at Crogh Patrick to this very day. It is easy to imagine the old Druids walking round and round standing stones, sacred trees and other holy places whilst chanting. Some European temples have ambulatories (walk ways), believed to be used for this kind of contemplative processing. The temple remains unearthed at

Heathrow also featured this sacred passageway. It is very evocative to imagine a whole tribe going on a torch-lit procession around a holy site, chanting and singing in honour of the old gods.

Regardless of what went on thousands of years ago, the Gods can still be contacted and honoured in the 21st century. Rather than following an exact formula, the important thing is to commune with the Gods and find out what they want. This can be done through meditation, clairvoyance, divination and various other means.

Sadly, the British lack the very early literature that Greece, Rome and Egypt have about their ancient Gods. Our distant ancestors did not record their tales in written form. In fact, they don't even appear to have inscribed the names of their Gods on altars and monuments until the impact of Rome. By the time mystical stories of Britain and Ireland were being written, in the Dark Ages and Medieval periods, it was by Christian monks. There were still polytheists around Ireland at the early stage (far fewer in Wales and England), but anything that they may have written has not survived to modern times, or at least not yet been rediscovered (who knows what archaeologists may one day unearth?).

These written tales are not, as such, ancient Pagan myth. They are fusions of native Pagan, Christian, and Classical Pagan ideas (the latter stemming from the fact that the literati of Europe at that time were schooled in Romano-Greek writings[33] dating back to ancient times). Woven throughout this were other, more secular concerns; it was not unknown for histories written by the scribes of a particular abbey to favour, and perhaps glamorise, the ancestors of local noble families, or to besmirch the ancestors of some rival tribe. These days it is common to look at history with the *caveat lector* that it was written by the victors. We might bear in mind not only who won, but also who financed the production of those historical records and quite what they expected to get for their money.

Thus we no longer know how the written fusion-myths compare to those stories being told before the coming of the missionaries[34]. Some of the Welsh tales do mention places outside the political boundaries of Wales, such as the dragons that dwelt beneath Oxford in 'Lludd and Llefelys'. However, those modern Druids living in most of England and Cornwall no longer have even fused myths to draw upon. Whatever songs were sung by the Iceni, Atrebates and Brigantes have long faded into almost complete silence. Some episodes within stories are very obviously Christian, such as the introduction of Biblical figures, whilst much of the rest is so dovetailed as to be impossible to pull apart (and there are many people who would not wish to do so anyway).

Heathens are, for once, in much the same position as Druids on this matter, given that their Eddas and other myths were also committed to parchment by Christians (Saxo Grammaticus, Snorri Sturluson etc) living in a fused culture. At risk of mortifying the more elitist adherents of both traditions, the similarity of practice and culture between early Norse, Anglo-Saxon and Insular Celtic cultures is really quite marked. Perhaps one day we will see a greater degree of dialogue between the two faiths?

These accounts give a deep insight into the fused Christian-Pagan[35] culture of the era in which they were written. As a window into the Iron Age, to purloin someone else's book title, they offer a much dimmer view. What they do highlight is the great importance placed upon the Pagan culture by many members of the Christian one. Christianity has had its loathsome book burners[36], and doubtless still has such characters skulking amidst its ranks. However, it has also had people who have bent over backwards to preserve what others would have carelessly destroyed. An evangelical crank could simply have stamped out all traces of an unwritten polytheist religion, yet clearly there were a sizeable number of abbots, bishops and other dignitaries who directed their scribes to preserve old tales.

As may be expected, biblical writings and hagiographies are likely to have been the most-esteemed form of literature in the eyes of an abbot. That they opted to fuse their beloved ecclesiastical writings with those strange and magical old tales says something about just how important they considered the stories and histories preserved by their polytheist grandparents to be. When St Patrick encountered the ghost of Fintan, a jaded eye could interpret it as clerical imperialism staking a claim on a glorious past, or (from a more optimistic view) it may be a sign of the scribe wanting to unite his equally beloved cultural icons in a harmonious tapestry.

Those stories recorded a thousand or more years after mass conversion may have been written down by people who had no idea that they were anything other than historical tales ~ they may not have understood that some of these strange characters were once considered Gods, but genuinely have thought of them as warriors, queens and court magicians.

An example of a less obvious influence is the story of Lugh's battle with Balor. It ends with Lugh killing the giant with a slingshot, which some historians feel might be the monks trying to create their own version of the David and Goliath tale. They may have added that story entirely, or they may have just changed the weapon in a pre-existing tale to make it more "biblical", or it may just be a coincidence that the Irish legend is vaguely similar to the old Hebrew story. Historians just don't know... though most historians do not actually believe Lugh exists, so it may explain why they do not consider actually asking Him if He approves of the tale.

A question that may occur to many readers is whether or not they should read the myths if they have such a strong Christian flavour. My answer to this is not a straightforward one, and probably not very helpful. As mentioned earlier in the book, I did try to find some demographic statistics about modern British Pagans. I can only speculate as to which socio-economic brackets most Pagans occupy, but I suspect the majority work hard for a living. Therefore their free time will be markedly limited. It seems unreasonable to ask people to invest what little time they do have reading something that seems so heavily tied to a frequently hostile monotheistic creed. Will someone staggering home from a mind numbing day at the factory or office really want to wade through densely written tales of the saints and sinners from a religion they may have had very bitter experiences of?

There is an immense beauty to these literary creations, one of great appeal not only to Christians but also to storytellers, historians and people with a passionate Welsh or Irish national identity. Pagans who also happen to be one of these things may well embrace the fusion-myths regardless of their Christian content. Pagans who are not any of those things may opt to spend their spare time in search of pre-monotheist accounts of the Gods, be that in a Celtic context or eschewing it for some better-documented culture[37]. In this regard there can be no surprise that many people may want to focus limited resources on doing something that they hope will generate a revolutionising spiritual bond to their Gods, rather than invest their efforts with something seen as too tied up with a monotheist culture.

This is also where we return to the issue of theology, which is not merely a pastime for the bored and bearded. Those Pagans following a Neoplatonist approach of all gods being One God will clearly have few difficulties finding mystical revelations in texts as much (or more) Christian as Pagan. Those of us who are polytheists will have no expectation that the truths revealed by Gobanos or Brigantia will be the same as those granted by Jehovah. Ancient polytheists often had little or no problem with accepting the existence of Jesus, Mary, Jehovah and assorted saints as just yet more Spirits in the vast and burgeoning Otherworld. As such many included icons to theoretically monotheist entities on altars alongside unashamedly polytheist figures, effectively demoting the One True God to one star amongst a constellation.

The intervening centuries of oppression and bloodshed on both sides have created rifts that may never heal. Whilst some 21ˢᵗ century polytheists are not alarmed at interacting with Christian icons or finding value in their mystical texts, others might easily be alienated by that religion's more odious attitudes.

Whether modern polytheists embrace these particular histories or not, it is vital for them to build relationships directly with the Gods; allow them to speak to you directly, rather than relying on any intermediary to do it for you.

Whilst meandering on the topic of tales, it is worth pausing briefly to look at the matter of language. All languages change over the centuries. To give an example, here are three short quotes all from English literature:

... if gold ruste, what shal iren doo?
For if a preest be foul, on whom we truste,
No wonder is a lewed man to ruste;
And shame it is, if a prest take keep,
A shiten shepherde and a clene sheep.
Geoffrey Chaucer (writing in the late 1300's)

Thou do him lowly homage for the same.
And for that purpose here I somon thee,
Repaire to France within these forty daies,
That there according as the coustome is,
Thou mayst be sworne true liegeman to our King
William Shakespeare (writing two centuries later, in1596)

You seek for knowledge and wisdom, as I once did; and I ardently hope
that the gratification of your wishes may not be a serpent to sting you,
as mine has been
Mary Shelley (writing just over 200 years later, in 1818)

In Chapter Three we discussed the names of the Gods, how the names used for them in the Iron Age changed over the centuries as language itself mutated. For those keen on reverencing these Gods, it is worth pausing to make a conscious decision about which names you wish to address Them by (or sitting and meditating to hear what names They want you to address Them by!). Will you toast Lugh or Lugus, or do you feel it makes no great difference which name you speak? This, in itself, is a question of theological importance to a polytheist ~ who names the Gods? Are these just fairly random titles dreamed up by mortal minds, or are they potent sounds spoken by the Gods? As intimated in an earlier chapter, in some cultures to speak certain words is to transform the mind of both speaker and listener. We just raise the question here; we don't aim to offer you answers!

Having briefly considered the nature of what makes a nemeton sacred; let us give some consideration to the nature of the wider Land. The Irish have a 12th century book, composed of histories and poems found in various manuscripts[38] some sections of which date back to the 800's, called the *Lebor Gabála Érenn* (The Book of the Takings of Ireland). When the early versions of these tales were being written down there were still a few Pagans left in Ireland, some of whom may have been known to the scribes.

The *Lebor* explains how five waves of invaders arrived in Ireland. The land was initially really quite small, but each wave created plains, lakes, mountains etc. Many of the references in the *Lebor* are picked up on in the *Dindsenchas*, a book full of topographical lore explaining how various landscape features got their names or were created by one mythical character or another. The monks who wrote this down believed they were recording actual history, which begs the question of what history actually is. These days we have the notion of history as an objective, independent record of things that can be proved to have actually happened. History is now a secular, academic concept, but has not always been so. Tribal non-literate cultures often fuse records of actual events with mythical accounts of gods, monsters and magical deeds. In doing so they do not necessarily see any conflict or distinction between both strands. Records of a battle may sit happily alongside references to humans having descended from wolves, both being regarded as truth. Without getting too pretentious, one may be seen as the truth of the conscious mind and the other of the unconscious.

Irish and Welsh myths both embody this fusion of factual and imaginative history. Sometimes the demarcation is hard to draw, as with the seemingly fanciful account of the Milesians coming from Spain ~ 21st century genetic research now showing a connection between the tribes of Ireland and those of ancient Iberia.

In the *Gabála* the land itself was essentially created by the deeds of gods, spirits, heroes and other magical characters. One particular episode involving the *Fir Bolg* is worth particular attention. However, we will give the general outline of the various arrivals and colonisations:

First a woman called Cesair sailed to Ireland (which was very small then) along with her father, two male friends and 149 women. The men each took a third of the women, and divided the land up between each small tribe. Cesair's father died of exhaustion (all those women!). His wives were then married off to the other two men, one of whom who also died from the strain. The third man, Fintan, naturally enough panicked and ran away. Cesair was grief-stricken and, as a result, a huge flood swept across the land and drowned all the women. Fintan survived by turning into a salmon.

The second wave was lead by a chieftain called Partholon, who arrived 312 years later at the feast of Beltaine, when the flood receded. Fintan turned into a hawk, so he could sit and watch what happened. The followers of Partholon expanded the land, made fields, dug lakes and invented all sorts of human activities ~ like brewing and animal husbandry. They also had the first murder committed amongst them! They were all eventually wiped out by a plague, again on the feast of Beltaine.

The third lot arrived 30 years later, and were the tribe of Nemed. They expanded the land still further, introduced more skills, and got attacked by underwater monsters called the *Fomóiri*. Their war against the monsters, which enslaved them and imposed terrible taxes, culminated in a huge battle that was ended by a tidal wave that drowned nearly everyone. Some *Fomóiri* survived, and slithered off into the sea. Some *Nemedians* survived, and went their separate ways ~ some to Britain, whilst some travelled the world.

The fourth wave was the Fir Bolgs, whose name may originate from the name of a continental tribe called the Belgae (who lived in what is now Belgium). They were descended from those *Nemedians* who went travelling the world. They arrived at Lughnasadh, and did similar things to the previous lot. Arguably their most important act was to divide Ireland into five provinces or *cuigeadh* (plural form of *coiced*), which was pretty much how the country was run until the Normans invaded it in the 12th century. The five sons of King Dela split the land between themselves. Initially Munster was considered to be in two parts for political and administrative purposes, though always treated as one big province in poetry and myth. The area of Meath was a symbolic fifth, seat of the High Kings. The four main provinces held the real power between them. The division of the land was a constant feature of myth and law, the *Fir Bolg* founders of each territory being:

Rudraighe, founder of Ulster,
Genann, founder of Connaught,
Slaine, founder of Leinster,
Sengann and Gann, joint-founders of Munster

Not far from the seat of Queen Medb in Connaught is the magical Cave of Cruachan, or *Uaigh na gCat* as it is often called these days.

A short way from this cave-entrance to the Otherworld is both the *Coirthe Dearg*, a red stone pillar supposedly marking the grave of the last Pagan king of Ireland (though it is probably much older than that) and a burial ground called *Relignaree*. This burial area is marked by a circular ring and divided roughly into quarters. Tradition has it that it is the burial place of the great heroes, and it may well be that the heroes of different provinces were buried in their own quarter.

The fifth wave brought the tribe of the goddess Danu, Anu or Anand, commonly called the *Tuatha Dé Danann*. They arrived at Beltaine, descending from the sky on clouds that caused a fog to spread across the land for three days. When the mists cleared, the Fir Bolg (and Fintan, still perched in a tree) were amazed to see their fortresses and palaces all built. Manuscripts disagree as to the location of the *Tuatha Dé's* arrival, but at least one version gives the Iron Mountain in County Leitrim. The scribes may have picked up on an old tradition of this being a sacred mountain, or they may have chosen it for other reasons. A number of cultures do have sacred mountains, such as Olympus ~ though the *Tuatha Dé* did not remain on the mountain but moved on to dwell at Tara. The *Tuatha Dé* came from the Otherworld, where there were four major fortresses (a Celtic fortress was basically a large village with a strong wooden palisade and sometimes a moat around it). Each fortress had its own Druid who, as a parting gift, presented the *Tuatha Dé* with a gift.

The fortress of Falias had a sage called Morfessa who gave a stone (maybe a monolith, but the actual size is never mentioned) that announces who the true kings of the new land are; the fortress of Gorias housed the wise man Esras who gave them a spear, which initially belonged to a god called Assal but eventually passed into the hands of Lugh, god of radiance (the spear is like a guided missile, always finding its target no matter how hard they try to hide, and returning on command); the fortress of Findias was home to Uscias who gave them the sword of light which was owned by Nuada, a god associated with healing and warfare ~ once unleashed, it always drew blood; finally the fortress of Murias had Semias who presented the Dagda with a magic cauldron that would produce whatever food the heart desired (but only as much as the individual deserved to have ~ dishonourable people getting virtually nothing).

Equipped with these magical gifts, the *Tuatha Dé* set about governing Ireland. The *Fir Bolg* refused to share the land, so a huge battle ensued. The *Fir Bolg* were defeated and agreed to live in the province of Connaught. All was well for a while, until the *Fomóiri* come back out from the bottom of the sea and attacked. The *Tuatha Dé* tried to make peace, and some even married the *Fomóiri*. However, the *Fomóiri* installed a bad king (who was half *Tuatha Dé*, half *Fomóiri*) who caused mayhem. Eventually the *Tuatha Dé* deposed him, and a second massive battle occurred. A great deal happened in this battle, but the important point was that the *Tuatha Dé* won.

Humanity arrived after a few centuries, under the leadership of a man called Mil. The *Tuatha Dé* agreed that humans could reign over the surface world, and that they would go and live in hollow hills and caves under the earth (beautiful caves, not grotty damp ones!).

There are other unusual stories contained within the Irish manuscripts, which encourage speculation. For example, a monastic scribe called Flann recorded a tale about the mythical building of Dowth. A bovine plague wiped out nearly all the cattle in Ireland, but Bresal managed to keep eight beasts in his herd. Perhaps as some sort of thanksgiving, he decided to build a great tower in emulation of Babel. For reasons not made clear, he insisted that the men of Ireland accomplish the building in a single day. Fortunately for them, Bresal's unnamed sister worked an act of *druídecht* (druid magic) to cause the sun to stand still. This could be a simple bit of phantasmagoria to liven up the story, or it may be an allusion to the solstice ~ the time when the sun stands still. Unfortunately Bresal became consumed with incestuous lust, and pounced on his sister. Though it is unclear, this may have disrupted the spell because the day rapidly came to an end, leaving the work undone. That is why, explained Flann, Dowth was not even higher.

This could be no more than a scribe inspiring a story to account for a landscape feature. It would be easy for those of us with overactive imaginations to draw parallels between this account and incest myths from around the world (where the first wave of deities often engage in incest in order to create the next generation). Storytellers, such as myself, find it hard to break the habit of seeing a couple of vague echoes and instinctively generating an entire saga around them. Even if there were once a Celtic myth about siblings shaping parts of the world, it is worth bearing in mind that there is no reason to suppose that the assorted tribes of ancient Ireland and Britain all shared the same stories. There could have been a dozen different origin myths doing the rounds of those early peoples.

This Christian-Pagan fusion story is not about the creation of the world, just about how Ireland developed. Some Christian fundamentalists may believe the story of Eden is absolutely true, but very few (if any) modern Druids believe that Celtic myths are real historical accounts. Rather they are stories, metaphors for understanding the world and the way the Gods and other spirits relate to each other, and to us. No direct parallel myth survives in the Welsh annals, but they were recorded at a late enough date that a great deal was doubtless lost. Whilst we cannot automatically assume that every Celtic tribe had similar myths, it is interesting to speculate as to the lost British creation myth. Did we once have tales about a wave of deities carving up the land into territories? If so, how many territories were there ~ five, or more? Maybe these territories, like the Irish ones, had patron gods and maybe the number was echoed in other tales (the way the four major provinces are echoed by the four cities of the *Tuatha Dé* and their four sacred Hallows)?

Alas we may never know the answers to these questions ~ unless the Land herself speaks to us, and we stop yapping long enough to listen.

Some questions for you to consider:

- When conducting solitary rituals, do you use the same level of ceremony as when working with others? Have you ever conducted or participated in a "public" ritual, where there were observers unfamiliar with what was happening? If so, did you change the nature of the ceremony in anyway?
- What are the legends associated with the place in which you live? How well do you relate to the locale, its stories and spirits?
- Can the holiness of a place be spoilt or desecrated? If so, how? If it can be violated, can it also be restored (and by what means)?

Practical exercise:

If you have completed this book and haven't totally lost interest in the topic, this is the time to leave the theory behind and start on the practice! Create your sacred space, choose the venue carefully and get on good terms with the spirits there. Conduct your first ritual ~ to mark the season, to honour the local spirits, or simply to celebrate Life itself.

A very simple ritual format is outlined below. Those readers with a Wiccan background may notice that there is no reference to the four elements of earth, air, fire and water. The notion of four elements stems from the Ancient Greek philosopher Empedocles. Whilst some Druids on the Continent almost certainly discussed cosmology over a pint of retsina with the occasional Greek philosopher (Pythagoras has already been mentioned earlier), we equally feel it unlikely that they would have chucked up their ancestral traditions in favour of an "exotic" idea popular amongst a distant peoples. We do not know quite what ancient Druids did at the start of their ceremonies, but it seems unlikely they would have been engaging in Greek (or Roman, Egyptian etc) practices.

The format below reflects the literary fascination with triads, and even if not especially ancient is certainly workable!

- Have a focal point for the ritual space, such as a sacred tree or a cauldron. Walk round this focus a set number of times (three, nine or some other multiple of the number three) whilst chanting a verse that seems suited to the ritual in hand. The *Carmina Gadelica* is full of inspirational verses (again a heavy fusion of Christian and Pagan ideas);
- Once the dizziness has passed, offer a libation in your own words to the local spirits;
- Then offer a libation in your own words to your beloved ancestors;
- Then offer a libation in your own words to the Gods whom you wish to honour in your ceremony;
- Conduct the main body of the ceremony in whatever manner you desire, then to draw the gathering to an end simply reverse the above gestures, giving your thanks to the spirits.

Afterword

Assuming you have been reading this book as part of your spiritual practice (rather than out of plain curiosity), you may well be wondering what to do now that it is all but finished. The book has, we hope, served as a springboard to launch you on to far more interesting possibilities. If you have followed the various exercises described, we can but hope that you now have formed (if you hadn't already) rewarding, transforming relationships with one or more deities and other spiritual beings. Having formed these relationships, you now have the rest of life in which to deepen them.

As you will have gathered by now, the amount that is known about the early polytheist religions of the Insular tribes is scant. The sizeable body of Irish and Welsh literature that has survived to present times was written by monotheists for monotheists (and is predominantly about monotheists). Fascinating as it is, it tells us about a period of time in which polytheism was dwindling away to virtually nothing. Those early texts from the 6th century[39] Ireland, when polytheists were still around, offer some gems about those people and their gods, but scarcely enough to construct a valid spiritual practice. By the time the Welsh and later Irish accounts were being penned, it is doubtful if there were any polytheists left in either land. Certainly not enough to have much of any influence over what was being recorded in monasteries.

Let me briefly drop the pretension of talking on behalf of a group, and spend a couple of paragraphs speaking one-to-one, author to reader. The word Druid (like the word Celt) has become iconic, conjuring up a rich array of different, dream-like images for different generations. Early on in this book I touched on some of those archetypes. For a great many people, myself included, one of the most potent draws of the icon is that of a priest of nature, the wise sage intimately bound to the spirituality of the Land in which he dwells. I won't rehash the historical veracity of this image, merely state it as a myth that inspires in the here and now.

Having written (and rewritten) this book, one of the strongest emotions I am left with is the sense of loss. Professional academics of whatever sort are usually encouraged[40] to maintain a sense of neutrality and distance, to advance or discard ideas on the strength of research rather than emotional investment. Amateurs, in whatever field, tend to find emotionalism much harder to resist. That may explain why the Internet is such a hotbed of people screeching at each other when their favoured idea is rejected or critiqued.

Coming from an academic background (in Psychology), I am used to relinquishing old theories and accepting new ones for which there is better evidence. Nonetheless, letting go of so much over the last five years[41] has been very difficult and I cannot honestly say that what I see growing in its place fills me with any sense of euphoria. When I very first started looking into Druidry, many years ago, there was the hope that I would find in it a wealth of lore about an ancient religion (and that that religion would be enlightening, liberating, awe-inspiring and magnificent). One of the theories discarded along the journey has been the belief that there was enough information left to even know if the religion of those ancient sages was any of those wonderful things in the first place.

The things I most valued as a younger man (and still value now) seemed to coalesce in the mythic image of the Druid ~ that love of cool forests and the stunning beasts that once dwelt amongst them; poetry and storytelling celebrated as devotional, spiritual acts; a belief in the sapience of other living, non-human creatures; responsible hedonism which relishes rather than abnegates life; and (purely self-interest, this one) the celebration of same-sex love as equally valid as heterosexual love. I am not saying that the ancient Druids and their tribes never expressed these ideals, only that we cannot now prove it and so to argue one way or the other really gets us nowhere. As stated several times previously, the body of magical tales that we draw upon largely shows us the workings of medieval Christian minds, and what they believed about their Pagan ancestors. Those histories do not prove that their beliefs were accurate.

Much of what went in to this book was part of a quest to find all those things in an idealised past. If those things ever existed in one group of learned mystics, then the evidence for it has long since gone. The hope of finding it has had to go by the wayside too. Before I get too maudlin, I want to return to one of the statements at the beginning: myth inspires the future. A romantic past that just leads one to gawping passively into dreamland is of little use. A vision of the future that inspires us to strive forward, to make that ideal a reality, is far more practical.

The tendency to place so much reliance on something that does not give direct access to what so many Pagans search for probably stems, at least in part, from a yearning for viability. Some religions take Divine Revelation as the mandate to validate their views for the way society should run. Few, if any, polytheists have tablets of stone or emerald inscribed with a deity's guidelines for how we should all be behaving. Lacking this basis, some of us scout around for alternate weight to add to whatever arguments we are making. The past is one such source ~ if an idea has been tried and tested before, then it gives it added credence (and reassurance to the person advancing the argument that what succeeded once could succeed again). The authors of the American Constitution may have argued for self-evident truths, but in these days of cacophonous squabbling there seems little, if anything, which can truly be called self-evident to all and sundry.

There are parallels that strike me quite strongly between the modern Druid's search for a positive past on which to found their present, and a similar quest amongst many gay people. A lot of rather romanticised histories are created about the place of gay men and women in ancient cultures, perhaps most especially Ancient Greece, much of which serve similar goals ~ to show modern audiences a world in which we were not scorned or hated or outlawed; to give ourselves a sense of having been worth something once. Many readers may suggest that self-worth is the only, or primary, factor of importance: if an individual values him/herself, what does it matter what others think? The rampant individualism of the modern West tends to close its eyes to the dominant role played by society. When others can shape laws, or engage in street "justice", then their opinions matter very much. To be valued by ones tribe (in whatever capacity) is to be safe.

If a positive identity existed once, it forms a bedrock on which to rebuild in the present. Besides, most people need upbeat stories about whichever group they identify with. We are a narrative species, with a natural inclination to create bonding stories where none previously existed.

If you are wondering why I still bothered to join with others to write about modern Druidry, it is because I am convinced of the existence of the Gods. Whether the ancient religion centred about them was amazing or not, those Gods are astounding entities and a new spirituality could be built around them that would be enlightening, liberating, awe-inspiring and magnificent.

If the world had never had a body of polytheist naturalists, seeing meaning and beauty and sapience in the land around them, then the 21st century would be a fantastic time for it to gain one. When has humanity ever been so in need of shutting its collective mouth long enough to actually hear what the other inhabitants of this planet are trying to say to it?

Curiously, whilst I was quite prepared to put a tremendous amount of work into searching for a glorious past, I cannot work up anywhere near as much enthusiasm for the amount of work it will take to make a decent future. Maybe I am just allowing pessimism about humanity's future to gain ascendancy! We cannot and should not reject the past, though understanding how modern Pagans now relate to it requires serious debate.

As said several times already, we have but a few nuggets of the Insular pre-Christian past left to us ~ and these are seldom, if ever, clear and easily understood. Some have been mentioned in this book: the day of *erdathe*; the five-fold metaphysical pattern of the provinces; statue bearing processions etc. These are scarcely enough to found a modern religion upon, unless they are both enthused and infused with a vivid and contemporary connection to the Gods, ancestors and other spirits.

Earlier in the book we mentioned the possibility of a ritual or celebration that may once have been held to mark the transition of a *filí* from the grade of *Fochlac* to that of *Mac Fuirmidh*. If you want to consider this book to be a sort of introductory course to a polytheist take on Druidry, then reading it (and understanding it, and completing the practical exercises etc) could be seen as coming to the end of that first tier. As with any kind of graduation, it provides an ideal chance for a bit of pomp and ceremony (not to mention a bun fight afterwards). Exactly how you do it is up to you, but the format we like to use within our group is inspired by the riddling contests featured in a number of Irish myths where a challenger poses a question, the response to which is always prefixed 'Not hard!' Each person in the group poses a question to the candidate, based upon the various topics they have been studying. If the candidate answers in a satisfactory manner to each question, their knowledge is considered to have been adequately demonstrated. The Gods are then invited to express an opinion through divination, and some symbolic gift is presented to represent the person's accomplishment.

Some readers may already be in Druid groups, and others have no desire at this time to join one. Other readers may be contemplating forming a ritual group; if you fall into this category we would advise you to gain a lot more experience before doing so. Reading a book is insufficient a foundation to form a group on.

Having taken your study this far, there are many more topics you might want to venture into:

- Studying a Celtic language is always rewarding, and can prove helpful when studying the old myths;
- Museum visits are always a good idea, to help you learn about the various waves of people who have left their mark on the place you now live in. As well as seeing their relics, you may be lucky enough to live in an area that has sites from the Neolithic, Iron Age, Roman, and Saxon or later periods. Whilst the focus of this book has been on the Iron Age, it is advisable to have an understanding of all the cultures that have influenced your area in the time between then and now;
- The Druids of old were considered students of the natural sciences, and you may well want to take a course in botany, astronomy, zoology or some other related area;
- Theory is fine, but hopefully you will want to apply the knowledge in a practical manner. In the case of the natural sciences, you might get involved with environmental preservation projects, volunteer at an animal sanctuary, or something of that sort;
- If of an artistic bent, you could create a whole raft of different visual arts or study the harp, *bodhran*, Irish "gob music" as it is so charmingly nicknamed etc;
- As well as feeding the soul, feeding the body is also important. Brewing, cooking ancient recipes or dishes beloved of your more recent ancestors, welcoming friends and spirits into your home are all courses worth pursuing;
- Meditation and spiritual communion are vital to maintain your links with the people of the Otherworld. Like any friendship, a mystical connection needs regular visits and exchanges of gifts to maintain. In a previous chapter, the idea of a Divine Patron or *flaith* was mooted. The reader may already have such a link

but, if you do not, this is not something to rush into. A deity will make contact in his or her own good time and, as is the nature of *lánamnas*, mutual benefits will arise.

Whatever you do, try and enjoy it. Learning should be a joy, not a chore, and ours is a religion that celebrates the fun things in life.

Appendix 1

Irish & Welsh Pronunciation Guide

Airmid	**ar**-ivið *
Annwn	**ann**-oon (*'oo' as in book*)
Awen	**ow**-en (*'ow' as in cow*)
Cailleach	**cal**'yukh
Dagda	dagh-ða *
Derbfine	dyervinyuh
Dian Cecht	**dee**-un **kekht**
Druí	dree
Erdathe	earth-other
Fáith	farth (*like the way Southern Brits say bath!*)
Feda	feða *
Fid	fið *
Fith-fáth	fee-fawh
Filí	filyee
Fine	finyuh
Imbas	**imm**-uss
Lugh	loo
Medb	meðv *
Óengus mac Óg	**oin**-guss muck **owg** (*'ow' as in mow*)
Ogma	**ogh**-vuh
Sídhe	shee
Tarbfeis	**tarv**-esh
Tuan mac Cairill	too-un muck **car**-ill
Tuatha Dé Danann	too-ther **day dahn**-unn

* *The symbol ð represents a 'th' sound, as in wi<u>th</u> & <u>th</u>ing.*
Thanks for this guide go to Dr Mark Williams of Peterhouse, Cambridge.

Appendix 2

The Seven Grades of the *Filid*

This information is gathered from the "Sequel to the Crith Gabhlach" and relates to the practices of the by then Christian *filid*, though is probably based on older practices.

Rank	Required Learning
Fochlac (*speaker; orator; sprig of brooklime?*)	50 ogams; 10 dreachts (*compositions*); 6 dians (*difficulties / challenges*); 30 tales; The Uraicept na h-Eicsin and its Remenda
Mac Fuirmidh (*determined son*)	50 ogams; 6 philosophy lessons; 30 tales; poems (of an unspecified number)
Dos (*a sapling; a bush*)	50 ogams; 6 philosophy lessons; 40 poems; Principles of grammar
Cana (*singer; wolf cub*)	20 Eman poems (*birth*); 110 tales; More principles of grammar; The Bretha Nemed (*the Laws of Privileges*)
Cli (*a pillar*)	40 Nuath poems (*twins*); 30 tales; The Secret Language of the Poets (possibly sign language?)
Anruth (*a noble stream*)	The Brosnacha (*miscellanies*); The art of prosody; Glosses of strange words The prophetic arts of: Teimn Laeghda Imbas Forosnai Dicheltal do Chennibh The Dindsenchas (*tales of places*);

Duili Feda (*wisdom tales*);
Poetic styles of: Sennet (*chanting?*)
Luasca (*rocking / undulating*)
Nena (?)
Eochraid (*keys*)
Sruith (*streams*)
175 tales

Ollamh (*master*)   100 Anamuin poems (*spiritual?*);
120 Cetals (*orations*);
The Four Arts of Poetry;
175 tales

The *Ollamh* was a master of some 550 stories, and in excess of 200 poems!

Appendix 3

The Ogam Letters

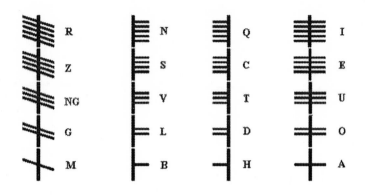

R	Ruis	Redness
Str/Z	Straif	Blackthorn? (Original meaning uncertain)
Ng	Ngetal	Broom
G	Gort	Hunger, also a field
M	Muin	The neck or throat

N	Nuin	Ash tree? (Original meaning uncertain)
S	Saille	Willow
F/V	Fearn	Alder
L	Luis	Flame, also an herb
B	Beith	Birch

Q	Quert	A rag/strip of cloth
C	Coll	Hazel
T	Tinne	An iron rod, or ingot
D	Duir	Oak
H	Huathe	Terror, wild fear

I	Iodho	Yew? (Original meaning uncertain)

E	Eadha	Poplar or aspen
U	Ur	Soil, the earth
O	Onn	Gorse or furze
A	Ailm	Pine? (Original meaning uncertain)

Footnotes

1 'Old Stones, New Temples', published by Xlibris.

2 God of knowledge, patron of historians, word-weavers and tale-spinners.

3 Available here:
   http://www.cyberwitch.com/wychwood/Library/whenIsACelt NotACelt.htm

4 Plus three sub-grades, so ten in all.

5 Caesar's description of an Arch-druid does suggest that some form of hierarchy existed. Though, of course, because the Pagan intelligentsia of one region organised in a certain pattern does not guarantee that those many miles away did the same.

6 The word *bard* appears in Gaelic as another form of poet, and may actually be older than the term *fili*. To avoid causing excessive confusion, we will generally use *fili* for the Gaelic poets and *bard* for the Welsh ones during the rest of this book.

7 Listed as wisdom, knowledge, counsel, fortitude, understanding, piety, and fear of the Lord.

8 We certainly hadn't quite twigged just how strongly tied to the Church this format was when gazing in awe at the lists of associated knowledge required of the various poetic tiers. Had we grasped the social context, would we have still gone for it? In all honesty I don't know. Some of our members may have happily gone along with a good idea regardless of whence it came, whilst others might have sooner drunk their own urine than participate in anything under the shadow of the crozier.

9 Can a deity behave badly? This depends on what one considers a deity to be in the first place. See Chapter Three for more thoughts on this topic.

10 Unless you are an astoundingly gifted linguist, we suggest you choose one and stick to it. The opportunities to actually use

such languages in everyday contexts are likely to be limited for anyone who lives outside of the Celtic nations (and often even within them). For the sake of practicality you might want to focus on learning how to pronounce names and say some simple blessings, as knowing how to order a plate of chips in Gaelic may prove to be a skill of limited use to someone living in Seattle or Berlin.

[11] Writing in *'The Conquest of Gaul'* in 50BCE.

[12] They may easily have been mistaken in their views, given the gap of time. Maybe other material will one day be unearthed that will help verify (or challenge) those monastic views.

[13] A 7th century law banned women from serving as warriors, though it is not clear for how long a period they had been doing so prior to this. Whether the women serving in this way were of a specific social class, or from all levels of society, is unknown.

[14] Please don't try this one at home! It leaves terrible stains on the carpet.

[15] Blagometry: the little known, but immensely useful, psychic ability to sense when someone else is talking or writing total tripe.

[16] Like any analogy, it falls flat if you carry it too far!

[17] Accessible here: http://www.manygods.org.uk/articles/essays/catanalogy.html.

[18] The genius in men, the juno in women.

[19] This applies regardless of whether we conceive of the beings in question as gods, sídhe, ancestral ghosts, totemic whatsits, huskies, Jack Russells, or even (at a push) other, still-living human beings.

[20] Which isn't to abnegate the wisdom to be had from studying taxonomy, just to point out that it is of secondary importance to the quality of the relationship.

[21] There is some linguistic contention over this equation, which is dealt with elsewhere in the book.

22 The word Ogmios, following linguistic rules, would have evolved into Égamh by the medieval period had it been present in Ireland from the Iron Age.

23 As already discussed, the Church became the keeper ~ and creator ~ of the official histories of Ireland, fusing Pagan traditions with Christian ones.

24 The person is called Maureen, obviously, and not the perm. Maureen would be a very silly name to give a perm.

25 An alternative argument is advanced by the authors of this Australian web site: http://caeraustralis.com.au

26 Remaining in the realm of the exceedingly speculative, Donn became lord of the Tech Duinn, Isle of the Dead, by himself falling overboard and drowning.

27 The 'De mirabilibus sacrae scripturae'.

28 The founder of this heretical school, Pelagius, was variously believed to be either Irish or British by birth and ran afoul of the ultra-zealous St Augustine.

29 'Saint Patrick, the Druids, and the End of the World', History of Religions, Vol 36, No. 1.

30 A book of this name, containing the medical lore, was translated by John Pughe and is now available from Llanerch Publishers.

31 Bearing in mind that many modern Druids take the story of Ogma carving the first set of symbols with his knife as a creation myth on a par with Odin finding the runes whilst dangling from Yggdrasil.

32 The state of being so impressed by the uses to which Heathens put their runes, that they are moved to seek out some equivalent system of their own.

33 Which were, in turn, heavily influenced by the learning coming out of Ancient Egypt and other African and Middle-Eastern cultures.

34 Prior to the missionaries both Britain and Ireland were cultures without any apparent written religious tales. Oral culture has

marked differences from manuscript culture (which is, in turn, different from our modern printed literacy). Literacy specialist Dr Richard Nokes wrote in his 2006 blog,

> *Textual cultural history to date can be divided into four different periods: oral culture, manuscript culture, print culture, and electronic culture.*

If you are interested in the distinctions between spoken and written lore, then Nokes is an excellent exponent to start with.

35 With the Pagan element no doubt getting smaller with each century that passed.

36 As has polytheism ~ think of that venal harridan incinerating the Sibylline Books to screw a higher price; or some of the religious tyrants from China's pre-Communist past.

37 I have known a few people lose heart with Druidry for the very reason that it is almost lost beneath the intervening layers of Christianity. Those people have gone on to find (one hopes) spiritual fulfilment in the arms of Gods from the literate cultures of Greece, Rome or Egypt. One or two remained quite scathing of neo-druidry; perhaps the embarrassed ire of reformed converts?

38 Such as the Book of Leinster, the Book of Ballymote, and the Great Book of Lecan.

39 Such as the *'Testament of Morann'* and the *'Auraicept na nEces'*.

40 Just because they are encouraged doesn't mean they all succeed ~ academics are human, after all, with the same range of passions and ideals as the rest of us.

41 It was about five years ago that we started created sets of notes for each class, though with no intention at that point of turning them into chapters in a book.

Recommended Reading

Freeman, P, *War, Women and Druids*, University of Texas Press, Austin, 2002, ISBN – 0292725450

Gantz, J (trans.), *Early Irish Myths and Sagas*, Penguin Classics, Middlesex, 1981, ISBN – 0140443975

Gregory, Lady A, *Lady Gregory's Complete Irish Mythology*, Bounty Books, London, 2005 reprint, ISBN – 0753709457

Handford, S (trans.), *Caesar, The Conquest of Gaul*, Penguin Classics, Middlesex, 1984 reprint, ISBN – 0140444335

Jones & Jones (trans.), *The Mabinogion*, Everyman, London, 1995 reprint, ISBN – 0460872974

Kinsella, T, *The Tain*, Oxford University Press, Oxford, 1969, ISBN – 0192810901

Koch, J and Carey, J, *The Celtic Heroic Age – 4th Edition*, Celtic Studies Publications, Aberystwyth, 2003 reprint, ISBN - 1891271091

Mackenzie, D, *Scottish Wonder Tales from Myth and Legend*, Dover Publications, New York, 1997 reprint, ISBN – 0486296776

MacKillop, J, *Dictionary of Celtic Mythology*, Oxford University Press, Oxford, 1998, ISBN – 0198691572

MacKillop, J, *Myths and Legends of the Celts*, Penguin Books, London, 2005, ISBN – 9780141017945

Patterson, N, *Cattle Lords and Clansmen – 2nd Edition*, University of Notre Dame Press, Indiana, 1994, ISBN – 0268008000

Power, P, *Sex and Marriage in Ancient Ireland*, Mercier Press, Dublin, 1997 reprint, ISBN – 1856350622

Restall-Orr, E, *Living with Honour*, O-Books, Winchester, 2007, ISBN – 9781846940941

Skelton, R, *Samhain*, Salmon Poetry, Dublin, 1994, ISBN – 1897648138

B O O K S

O is a symbol of the world, of oneness and unity. In different cultures it also means the "eye," symbolizing knowledge and insight. We aim to publish books that are accessible, constructive and that challenge accepted opinion, both that of academia and the "moral majority."

Our books are available in all good English language bookstores worldwide. If you don't see the book on the shelves ask the bookstore to order it for you, quoting the ISBN number and title. Alternatively you can order online (all major online retail sites carry our titles) or contact the distributor in the relevant country, listed on the copyright page.

See our website **www.o-books.net** for a full list of over 500 titles, growing by 100 a year.

And tune in to myspiritradio.com for our book review radio show, hosted by June-Elleni Laine, where you can listen to the authors discussing their books.

MySpiritRadio